Religious Fundamentalism

Hal Marcovitz

Current Issues

ReferencePoint
Press®

San Diego, CA

ReferencePoint Press®

About the Author:
Hal Marcovitz, a writer based in Chalfont, Pennsylvania, has written more than 100 books for young adult readers. His other titles in the Compact Research series include *Phobias, Hepatitis, Sleep Disorders, Bipolar Disorders,* and *Meningitis.*

© 2010 ReferencePoint Press, Inc.

For more information, contact:
ReferencePoint Press, Inc.
PO Box 27779
San Diego, CA 92198
www.ReferencePointPress.com

Picture credits:
Maury Aaseng: 33–36, 50–53, 68–70, 85–87
AP Images: 13, 16

LIBRARY OF CONGRESS CATALOGING-IN-PUBLICATION DATA

Marcovitz, Hal.
  Religious fundamentalism / by Hal Marcovitz.
    p. cm. — (Compact research)
  Includes bibliographical references and index.
  ISBN-13: 978-1-60152-082-1 (hardback)
  ISBN-10: 1-60152-082-4 (hardback)
  1. Religious fundamentalism. I. Title.
  BL238.M36 2009
  200.9'04—dc22
                                        2009000420

Contents

Foreword   4

Religious Fundamentalism at a Glance   6
Overview   8

How Widespread Is Religious Fundamentalism?   21
    Primary Source Quotes   28
    Facts and Illustrations   32

Does Religious Fundamentalism Threaten
  Individual Rights?   37
    Primary Source Quotes   45
    Facts and Illustrations   49

Does Religious Fundamentalism Fuel Violence
  and Terrorism?   55
    Primary Source Quotes   63
    Facts and Illustrations   67

How Should Governments Respond to Religious
  Fundamentalism?   71
    Primary Source Quotes   79
    Facts and Illustrations   84

Key People and Advocacy Groups   89
Chronology   92
Related Organizations   94
For Further Research   98
Source Notes   100
List of Illustrations   102
Index   103

Foreword

As modern civilization continues to evolve, its ability to create, store, distribute, and access information expands exponentially. The explosion of information from all media continues to increase at a phenomenal rate. By 2020 some experts predict the worldwide information base will double every 73 days. While access to diverse sources of information and perspectives is paramount to any democratic society, information alone cannot help people gain knowledge and understanding. Information must be organized and presented clearly and succinctly in order to be understood. The challenge in the digital age becomes not the creation of information, but how best to sort, organize, enhance, and present information.

ReferencePoint Press developed the *Compact Research* series with this challenge of the information age in mind. More than any other subject area today, researching current issues can yield vast, diverse, and unqualified information that can be intimidating and overwhelming for even the most advanced and motivated researcher. The *Compact Research* series offers a compact, relevant, intelligent, and conveniently organized collection of information covering a variety of current topics ranging from illegal immigration and deforestation to diseases such as anorexia and meningitis.

The series focuses on three types of information: objective single-author narratives, opinion-based primary source quotations, and facts and statistics. The clearly written objective narratives provide context and reliable background information. Primary source quotes are carefully selected and cited, exposing the reader to differing points of view. And facts and statistics sections aid the reader in evaluating perspectives. Presenting these key types of information creates a richer, more balanced learning experience.

For better understanding and convenience, the series enhances information by organizing it into narrower topics and adding design features that make it easy for a reader to identify desired content. For example, in *Compact Research: Illegal Immigration*, a chapter covering the economic impact of illegal immigration has an objective narrative explaining the various ways the economy is impacted, a balanced section of numerous primary source quotes on the topic, followed by facts and full-color illustrations to encourage evaluation of contrasting perspectives.

The ancient Roman philosopher Lucius Annaeus Seneca wrote, "It is quality rather than quantity that matters." More than just a collection of content, the *Compact Research* series is simply committed to creating, finding, organizing, and presenting the most relevant and appropriate amount of information on a current topic in a user-friendly style that invites, intrigues, and fosters understanding.

Religious Fundamentalism at a Glance

Defining Religious Fundamentalism

Religious fundamentalists believe in literal interpretations of their religious doctrines, meaning they believe the Bible, the Qur'an, or other holy scriptures word for word.

Prevalence

As many as 36 million Americans are members of fundamentalist Christian churches; Islamic fundamentalists may number 150 million worldwide. In India, fundamentalist Hindus number 4.5 million or more. Other major world religions also include fundamentalist elements.

The Appeal of Religious Fundamentalism

Fundamentalism may provide a safe haven from war, conflict, or rapid changes in society and technology.

Fitting into Modern Life

Concepts that form the basis of many fundamentalist notions are often centuries old and inflexible and do not change to accommodate contemporary ideas.

Individual Rights

Women and gays often lose their rights in societies controlled by fundamentalist ideologies.

Potential Dangers

Some fundamentalists turn to terrorism and other violent acts to spread their message; the September 11, 2001, terrorist attacks are the most prominent among many acts of terror prompted by the fervor of fundamentalists.

Fundamentalist Pacifists

The vast majority of religious fundamentalists preach messages of peace; some church members, including Mennonites, Seventh-Day Adventists, the Amish, and Jehovah's Witnesses, refuse to serve in combat.

Government Responses

In America, the courts constantly weigh the constitutional provision of freedom to worship against the requirement for a separation of church and state; in other countries, regimes often turn to force to control rebellious fundamentalists.

Overview

66 It is the unprecedented combined impact of fundamentalism in religion and politics that has helped to create the deep and increasingly disturbing divisions among our people. 99

—Jimmy Carter, former president of the United States.

66 Jesus Christ intended his church to be militant as well as persuasive. . . . Lord save us from off-handed, flabby-cheeked, brittle-boned, weak-kneed, thin-skinned, pliable, plastic, spineless, effeminate, sissified, three-caret Christianity. 99

—Billy Sunday, early twentieth-century fundamentalist preacher.

People who practice a fundamentalist form of their faith can be found in virtually every society on Earth. Fundamentalists believe in literal interpretations of their religious doctrines. In American society, fundamentalist Protestants believe in the concept of creationism. A strict and literal interpretation of creationism holds the belief that the world was created as the book of Genesis describes it: in six days; and that evolution—as Charles Darwin explained it—had nothing to do with the origin of the species. "And God made the beasts of the earth according to their kinds and the cattle according to their kinds," says the Bible in Genesis 1:25, "and everything that creeps upon the ground according to its kind. And God saw that it was good."

Moreover, fundamentalist Christians believe Earth was created between 6,000 and 10,000 years ago. Scientists and others who reject fundamentalist notions have a much different interpretation of the origins of Earth and life on the planet. They believe Earth coalesced from a cloud of dust, rocks, and gas during the birth of the solar system, and that the planet is at least 4 billion years old. They also believe the earliest forms of life, single-celled organisms, evolved on Earth 3.5 billion years ago.

With the scientific and religious communities holding such vastly different notions of how Earth formed and life evolved, on many occasions the two sides clash on the issue of evolution as well as other beliefs harbored by fundamentalists. In many cases American institutions such as the schools and courts are drawn into the argument, forcing people to weigh one constitutional provision, the freedom to worship, against another, which guarantees a separation of church and state.

In many other countries people harbor fundamentalist ideals and often find themselves clashing with their neighbors and governments. In Islamic societies, fundamentalists believe in a strict interpretation of sharia, the laws that govern Islamic life: how Muslims eat, dress, worship, and conduct themselves in relationships with others. (*Sharia* is an Arabic word that means "path.") As Americans and others have learned, some Islamic fundamentalists are willing to commit horrific acts of terrorism to spread their beliefs.

> " In many cases, American institutions such as the schools and courts are drawn into the argument, forcing people to weigh one constitutional provision, the freedom to worship, against another, which guarantees a separation of church and state. "

Fundamentalists in Mainstream Society

In America and elsewhere, it could be argued that fundamentalists represent a large and mainstream segment of society. In America, there may be 36 million or more fundamentalist Christians. Worldwide, the number of Muslims who harbor fundamentalist beliefs may total 150 million. Across the globe, millions of others practice fundamentalist versions of Judaism, Catholicism, Buddhism, and Hinduism.

Al Gore, a former vice president of the United States, believes people embrace fundamentalist religious principles to shield themselves against sudden change and upheaval in their societies. If their governments topple or go to war, or technology moves at too fast a pace for them to understand, Gore says, people often turn to religious principles that have remained unchanged for hundreds or even thousands of years. On the other hand, Gore says, as people cling closely to fundamentalist beliefs, they also risk rejecting new ideas that could bring positive changes to their lives:

> To brace themselves and their families against disturbing and disorienting change, people instinctively reach for the strongest tree they can find—which is often the one that seems to have the deepest roots. . . .
>
> If dogma and blind faith rush in to fill the vacuum left by reason's departure, they allow for the exercise of new forms of power more arbitrary and less derived from the consent of the governed. In simple terms, when fear and anxiety play a larger role in our society, logic and reason play a diminished role in our collective decision making.[1]

Concerns About Religious Fundamentalism

Because fundamentalists observe laws, customs, and rituals that often date back centuries or more, their ideals frequently clash with modern culture. In many parts of the world women have won equal rights, but in the Arab world a fundamentalist interpretation of the sharia and Qur'an, the book of Islamic laws, does not accept women as equals with men. In America fundamentalist Christians often see popular culture as a threat to their beliefs—they often denounce pop music, explicit films, revealing fashions, and edgy art as un-Christian.

Fundamentalists have bristled at the success of the books and movies chronicling the adventures of boy wizard Harry Potter. Since 1997, when the character was first introduced, titles in the series have sold 400 million copies while the films have chalked up a staggering worldwide box office gross of nearly $5 billion.

Since publication of the original title, *Harry Potter and the Sorcerer's Stone*, fundamentalist Christians have warned that the series teaches an appreciation for witchcraft and pagan beliefs. In 2007 series author J.K. Rowling disclosed that Dumbledore, the beloved headmaster of Harry's school, is gay, a lifestyle rejected by fundamentalists as a violation of what they regard as the moral code that guides Christians. Soon after Rowling's disclosure, fundamentalist leaders renewed their calls for parents to keep the books out of the hands of their children. Fumed Jack M. Roper, a commentator on Christian Broadcasting Network, "No one in my family will ever read that trash again."[2]

Does Religious Fundamentalism Threaten Individual Rights?

In some societies fundamentalists have enormous influence because their principles have been adopted by their governments. In Saudi Arabia, the ruling family practices a fundamentalist form of Islam known as Wahhabism, first preached by eighteenth-century Islamic scholar Muhammad ibn-Abdul Wahhab. All other public worship in Saudi Arabia is prohibited—an infringement on the rights of the 3 million non-Muslims who live and work in the kingdom. Christians who live in Saudi Arabia are prohibited from displaying Christmas decorations. Even the public practice of more progressive forms of Islam is prohibited. Said Ali al-Ahmed, a Saudi expatriate and director of the Washington-based Institute for Gulf Affairs, "[Saudi Arabia] is the world headquarters of religious oppression."[3]

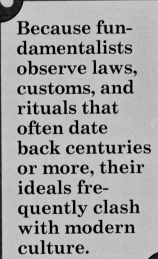

> Because fundamentalists observe laws, customs, and rituals that often date back centuries or more, their ideals frequently clash with modern culture.

The Saudi law is upheld by the government's Commission to Promote Virtue and Prevent Vice, a religious police force whose officers are armed with whips. The religious police may lash citizens whom they find in violation of the country's strict interpretation of sharia. In one case, a woman found alone in a car with a man who was not her relative was sentenced by a Saudi court to

200 lashes and six months in prison. Saudi king Abdullah intervened to pardon the woman but also confided that he believed the sentence was justified.

> **❝**
>
> In one case, a woman found alone in a car with a man who was not her relative was sentenced by a Saudi court to 200 lashes and six months in prison.
>
> **❞**

Jailed for Blasphemy

Saudi Arabia is a kingdom where Abdullah rules as a near-absolute monarch. Even in democracies, people can see their rights erode under fundamentalism. Afghanistan has been a democracy since 2004, soon after American-led forces ousted the fundamentalist Taliban regime, which harbored the terrorists responsible for the September 11, 2001, attacks on the World Trade Center and Pentagon.

Nevertheless, fundamentalist Islamic leaders still maintain influence in the country. In 2008 Afghan journalist Sayed Parwiz Kamakhsh was sentenced to prison for publishing articles against Islam deemed blasphemous in which he called for expansion of women's rights. In other words, he questioned the teachings of Muhammad, the seventh-century prophet who first repeated the words of the god Allah that evolved into the tenets of Islam. Under Afghan law, Kamakhsh's right to a trial was severely limited. He was held in jail during the proceedings and given limited access to a lawyer. "He was detained far longer than he should have been legally held," insisted John Dempsey, an American attorney who observed the trial. "The defense lawyer was not even allowed to meet the witnesses until a night before the trial."[4]

Afghan justice can be particularly harsh on blasphemers. Kamakhsh was originally sentenced to die, but an appeals court overturned the sentence and reduced his penalty to 20 years in prison.

Political Influence

In democratic societies fundamentalists often call on the numerical strength of their memberships to sway elections and influence public policy. In America fundamentalist Christian leaders oppose abortion rights, which are guaranteed under the U.S. Supreme Court's 1973 *Roe v. Wade* decision. During the 1990s fundamentalists often blocked entrances to abortion clinics. Even though federal law made it illegal to block abortion clinic entrances in 1994, protests have continued, and many clinic staff members and clients feel intimidated by antiabortion activists, many of whom are members of fundamentalist churches. In Mississippi, a state

In America, there may be 36 million or more fundamentalist Christians. The fundamentalist Christian leaders oppose abortion rights, which are guaranteed under the U.S. Supreme Court's 1973 Roe v. Wade *decision. Flip Benham (standing with bible), the director of Operation Save America, leads a group of antiabortion supporters in prayer in front of an abortion clinic.*

with a large fundamentalist Christian population, strict state laws regulate abortion, and just one abortion clinic is in operation.

In 2006 antiabortion activists staged a protest in front of that clinic, which is located in the city of Jackson, hoping to convince clients to stay away. Said the Reverend Flip Benham, director of the national antiabortion rights group Operation Save America, "This is a grassroots battle that will be won by the gospel of Jesus Christ."[5] In this case the public campaign fell short, and the Jackson Women's Health Organization clinic remained open despite the protest.

Does Religious Fundamentalism Fuel Violence and Terrorism?

The terrorist group responsible for the September 11 attacks is known as al Qaeda. It is headed by Osama bin Laden, a wealthy Saudi who embraced fundamentalist Islam in the 1980s when he served in Afghanistan as a mujahid, an armed defender of Islam. Bin Laden and other Muslims volunteered to help the Afghan guerillas expel the army of the Soviet Union, which had invaded Afghanistan in 1979. The Soviets endured a decade of guerilla warfare, finally leaving Afghanistan in 1989. Bin Laden and other radical Islamists saw themselves as soldiers in a jihad, or holy war, waged to rid sacred Islamic territory of nonbelievers, whom they call infidels.

> " In democratic societies, fundamentalists often call on the numerical strength of their memberships to sway elections and influence public policy. "

For Bin Laden and other radicals, the ejection of the Soviets from Afghan soil did not end what they perceived as an international threat against Islam. As they looked elsewhere in the world, they saw infidels—and in particular, Americans—degrading the holy soil of their religious homelands by introducing Western customs into Islamic nations.

On October 12, 2000, a small boat approached a U.S. Navy vessel, the USS *Cole,* as it was anchored off the coast of Yemen, a country located along the southern tip of the Arabian Peninsula. Suddenly, the boat exploded, blasting a huge hole in the side of the *Cole.* The blast killed 17 crew members and injured 40 others. Al Qaeda took credit for the act of terrorism.

The attack on the *Cole* served as stark evidence that radical Islamic fundamentalists represent an international menace. The incident is regarded as the first strike by al Qaeda to drive Americans off the Arabian Peninsula; depose the ruling Saudi family, whom al Qaeda regards as American pawns; and establish an Islamic ruler known as a caliph to protect the holy cities of Mecca and Medina. Other terrorist strikes by al Qaeda, including the attacks of September 11, would follow. Today, al Qaeda leaders remain in hiding as American troops occupy Afghanistan, searching for Bin Laden and other leaders of the terrorist group.

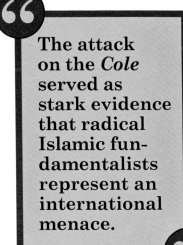

The attack on the *Cole* served as stark evidence that radical Islamic fundamentalists represent an international menace.

Assassination as a Tool of Fundamentalism

Fundamentalists have used assassination to advance their agendas. Among the heads of state murdered by fundamentalists are Indira Gandhi, prime minister of India, who was assassinated by fundamentalists of the Sikh faith; Egyptian president Anwar Sadat, murdered by radical Islamists after signing a treaty with Israel; and Israeli prime minister Yitzhak Rabin, shot and killed by a fundamentalist Jew who opposed Rabin's peace overtures to the Palestinians.

In all cases the governments of those nations stabilized after the murders, thwarting the fundamentalist causes that prompted the assassinations. In Israel national leaders worry that as they continue to pursue peace with the Palestinians, the radical fundamentalists will again turn to assassination as the method of achieving their goal. "The seed of calamity has already been sown; it has been sown in messianic groups," says former prime minister Ehud Barak. "They aren't many, but like a cancerous growth they are deadly. We must not ignore this and must work to uproot it."[6]

In late 2007 Pakistani prime minister candidate Benazir Bhutto was assassinated by Islamic extremists who opposed the progressive-minded reformer. Soon authorities identified Baitullah Mahsud, a Pakistani leader of the former Taliban regime, as the prime suspect in Bhutto's murder.

Elsewhere, assassination remains a tactic employed in some of the world's most volatile corners. In late 2007 Pakistani prime minister candidate Benazir Bhutto was assassinated by Islamic extremists who opposed the progressive-minded reformer. Bhutto was killed by suicide bombers who approached her car at a political rally, then detonated a powerful explosive that killed themselves as well as the candidate. Soon authorities identified Baitullah Mahsud, a Pakistani leader of the former Taliban regime, as the prime suspect in Bhutto's murder. Investigators intercepted a telephone conversation in which Mahsud says, "They were brave boys who killed her."[7]

As with the incidents in Egypt, Israel, and India, Mahsud's effort to destabilize the country failed. Shortly after Bhutto's murder, her widower, Asif Ali Zardari, was elected president of Pakistan.

Terror in the Name of Christ

Terrorist activities in America often emerge from radical extremist groups whose hatred of nonwhite races and non-Christian faiths can be traced to their twisted interpretations of the Bible. Such hate groups as the Covenant, the Sword and the Arm of the Lord (CSA), the Army of God, and the World Church of the Creator have committed acts of terror in the United States.

These groups adhere to a philosophy they call "Christian Identity," which suggests the Bible's book of Revelation has predicted future events. According to the prophecies of the book of Revelation, Christ will return to Earth, summoning true believers to heaven. Christ's reappearance on Earth is known as the Rapture. Nonbelievers will be left behind, where they will be swallowed up in a tumultuous seven-year period known as the Tribulation that will feature wars, plagues, floods, and meteor strikes. During this period, a third of the world's population will die. Finally, at the end of the Tribulation, God will defeat the devil, ushering in a 1,000-year era of peace.

> " Terrorist activities in America often emerge from radical extremist groups whose hatred of nonwhite races and non-Christian faiths can be traced to their twisted interpretations of the Bible. "

Members of the Christian Identity movement believe that to survive the Rapture, they must arm themselves and build fortified compounds. Some of their members have taken their campaigns of hate further, developing racist, anti-Semitic, and homophobic notions and targeting African Americans, Jews, and gays with acts of violence. In 2005 one of the most notorious of the Christian Identity terrorists, Eric Robert Rudolph, was sentenced to five life terms after pleading guilty to setting off a series of bombs targeting abortion clinics, a gay nightclub, and a crowded park in Atlanta, Georgia, where a concert had been held during the 1996 Summer Olympics. Two people died in the blasts. Says Idaho State University professor James A. Aho, an expert on Christian terror groups, "Religiously inspired terrorism is a worldwide phenomenon, and every major world religion has people who have appropriated the label of their religion in order to legitimize their violence."[8]

> " The Tangipahoa School District in Louisiana permitted Christian prayers during school events, such as classes, school board meetings, and football games. Responding to complaints from parents, the American Civil Liberties Union filed a series of lawsuits. "

How Should Governments Respond to Religious Fundamentalism?

In America the First Amendment to the U.S. Constitution guarantees separation of church and state. As such, it has often fallen on the courts to determine when fundamentalists have stepped over the line, and in fact, courts are constantly being asked to consider separation of church and state cases.

For years, the Tangipahoa School District in Louisiana permitted Christian prayers during school events, such as classes, school board meetings, and football games. Responding to complaints from parents, the American Civil Liberties Union (ACLU) filed a series of lawsuits, asking the court to bar school-sanctioned religious prayers during school events. In each case the court sided with the ACLU.

The latest suit was filed in 2007, after a teacher stood before the Tangipahoa graduating class and led a Christian prayer. Again, a judge ruled that the board had violated the First Amendment by sanctioning prayer at a school event.

The Use of Force

Occasionally, governments must act with force against their own people. As the Israeli and Palestinian governments try to resolve the issue of statehood for the Palestinian people, some of the most vehement opponents of an independent Palestine are fundamentalist Jews who occupy the West Bank settlement known as Kiryat Arba. Israeli police and soldiers have clashed with Jewish residents of the settlement, who vow never to leave the West Bank. The region, which Israel seized from neighboring Jordan during a 1967 war, would be turned over to the Palestinians under proposed statehood plans. Over the decades fundamentalist Jews have established settlements in the West Bank and now refuse to leave.

Elliot Jager, the editorial page editor for the *Jerusalem Post,* surveyed the ill will harbored by fundamentalist Jews against their own government—even finding that the fundamentalists have likened the soldiers of the Israeli army, known as the Israel Defense Force (IDF), to the Nazis who oversaw the Warsaw ghetto during World War II and the extermination of Polish Jews. In an essay, Jager wrote,

> In some countries, governments consider fundamentalists a threat to their power and have instituted crackdowns, jailing leaders and otherwise limiting their influence.

A process of demonization is taking place before our eyes. The Israel government—whatever its many faults—and the Israel Defense Force are denigrated as "un-Jewish." The nation watched in shock as Kiryat Arba rabbi Dov Lior compared the actions of the IDF in dismantling the settler outpost to the behavior of Nazi soldiers in occupied Poland. . . .

In recent weeks, masked, rock-throwing Jewish youths have fought with soldiers. Who on the right will denounce this despicable behavior?

I heard that radical parents are teaching their children that IDF soldiers sent to take down illegal structures aren't "real" Jews. . . . Others have prayed for IDF soldiers to be captured, defeated, even killed.[9]

Crackdowns Are Common

In some countries, governments consider fundamentalists a threat to their power and have instituted crackdowns, jailing leaders and otherwise limiting their influence. Before his ouster as president of Pakistan in 2008, strongman Pervaiz Musharraf often ordered arrests of fundamentalist leaders, including the leaders of conservative Islamic schools, or madrassas, that advocated Islamic revolution. Regimes that order crackdowns usually rule with strong-arm tactics. They may use torture, banishment, and murder to keep their restless citizens in check. In many cases those tactics run their course—history books are full of stories of despots who failed to recognize the growing power of fundamentalists.

In the early years of the twenty-first century, fundamentalists across the globe find themselves struggling to define their places in society. In America and elsewhere, they often engage in a test of wills as well as a test of political strength against others who believe strict religious principles have no place in the government, schools, or popular culture. In America these disputes are usually confined to courtrooms and legislatures. Nevertheless, some fundamentalists have been willing to use violent methods to achieve their goals, confident in the belief that they will eventually prevail because God is on their side.

How Widespread
Is Religious
Fundamentalism?

> **Fundamentalism is one of the most significant political phenomena of our time.**
>
> —Gabriel A. Almond, R. Scott Appleby, and Emmanuel Sivan, authors
> of *Strong Religion: The Rise of Fundamentalisms Around the World.*

> **We really are on the extreme fringe of society today. And that's our curse.**
>
> —Gary North, fundamentalist Christian author.

In America all faiths contain an element of fundamentalism, and in many cases fundamentalists represent a significant segment of the religion. According to the Pew Forum on Religion and Public Life, fundamentalists compose 59 percent of the membership of evangelical churches in America, which in turn account for 26 percent of the Protestant population of some 156 million people. Based on those statistics, about 24 million American fundamentalist Protestants belong to evangelical churches.

But the number of fundamentalist Protestants is likely larger than that because many fundamentalists belong to other Protestant traditions, including the Methodists, Lutherans, and Presbyterians, as well as black churches. The Pew statistics indicate that 22 percent of the members of other Protestant churches believe in the literal message of the Bible. That statistic would add another 6 million people to the total. And 62 percent of the members of black churches also regard themselves as fundamentalists, adding still another 6 million. In other words, about 36 million American Protestants believe in the literal message of the Bible.

Those are hefty numbers, and fundamentalists have often used the strength of their numbers to set church policy as well as influence society.

But Protestants make up about 51 percent of the American population— another 33 percent are members of other faiths, while about 16 percent of Americans consider themselves "unaffiliated" with organized religions.

As for members of other religions, fundamentalists often represent a small proportion of the members of their faiths—Hasidic Jews and members of similar fundamentalist sects compose just a fraction of American Jewry. Hasidic Jews restrict the culture and educations of their children along strict religious guidelines. Moreover, Hasidic Jews must dress conservatively, eat kosher food only, and marry other Hasidic Jews. Few Jewish congregations in America have adopted the cloistered lifestyles of Hasidism.

> **About 36 million American Protestants believe in the literal message of the Bible.**

As for fundamentalists in other countries, experts have provided some rough estimates of their numbers and influence. Daniel Pipes, an author, college professor, and critic of radical Islam, has estimated the worldwide population of Islamic fundamentalists at 150 million—about 10 percent of the international Muslim population. "These are Islamists, individuals who seek a totalistic, worldwide application of Islamic law, the Shari'a," says Pipes. "In particular, they seek to build an Islamic state in Turkey, replace Israel with an Islamic state and the U.S. constitution with the Koran."[10]

Because recent terrorist attacks have been perpetrated by Islamic fundamentalists, many Americans believe radical Muslims hold a large measure of influence over the Islamic faith, but mainstream Muslim leaders contend that that is not so. They point to many similarities between Islamic and Christian doctrines—belief in a single god, a requirement to love one's neighbors, and humility in dealing with others—that prove Islam is a faith with a peaceful message.

Growth of the Megachurches

In America some fundamentalist congregations have established churches that seat thousands of worshippers. The churches offer their congregants more than a place for Sunday worship. Many feature athletic fields and gyms, stores, arcades, classrooms, and other facilities that make the churches the centers of their communities. On Sundays preachers deliver sermons to audiences of 2,000 or more. The number of "megachurches" in America is estimated to be at least 900, and many of them adhere to fundamentalist doctrines.

The largest of the megachurches is the 47,000-member Lakewood Church of Houston, Texas. Lakewood is a Pentecostal denomination. Pentecostals have adopted many fundamentalist principles, including a literal interpretation of the Bible as well as the concept of biblical inerrancy, meaning they believe the Bible is free of error and contradiction. Lakewood's congregation is so large that to accommodate Sunday worshippers the church acquired the arena that formerly housed the NBA's Houston Rockets. Each Sunday Lakewood's ministers lead services before an audience of some 16,000 worshippers.

Growth of Radical Islam

In the Middle East, modern fundamentalist Islam can trace its roots to the founding of the Muslim Brotherhood in Egypt in 1928. Since its inception, the brotherhood has been committed to establishing the Qur'an as the universal law for all Islamic states. In the past, members of the brotherhood used violence to achieve their goals.

Over the years radical Islamists mostly operated on the fringes of Muslim society, but in 1979 the American-backed shah of Iran was deposed by an Islamic fundamentalist movement, leading to the establishment of an Islamic republic. Today, the mullahs who run Iran, a country of 65 million people, control every facet of Iranian life. They also control relations with foreign governments, which have often been icy because the fundamentalist regime's values clash with the progressive ideals that form the basis of modern Western societies.

> " Pentecostals have adopted many fundamentalist principles, including a literal interpretation of the Bible as well as the concept of biblical inerrancy, meaning they believe the Bible is free of error and contradiction. "

Courts in Iran operate under the country's conservative version of Islamic sharia law. This means women who have been raped are regarded as criminals because they have had sexual relations with men who were not their husbands. In most other societies, these women would be regarded as victims. In Iran they face death by stoning—a common sentence administered by Iran's Islamic courts. Says Iranian American attorney Lily Mazahery, "In 99 percent of these cases, the accused women have received no legal representation because, under the sharia legal system, their testimony is at best worth only half the value of the testimony of men."[11]

Men found to be in violation of sharia law also face death by stoning. In 1997 an Iranian man, Jafar Kiani, was arrested by authorities on the charge of committing adultery. He spent a decade in prison, and then in 2007 the courts finally carried out his sentence: death by stoning.

Catholic Fundamentalism

In America fundamentalists make up about 23 percent of the 64 million members of the Catholic faith, according to the Pew Forum. Despite their minority status in America and elsewhere, fundamentalist Catholics point out that recent popes have generally been conservative in their thinking and that fundamentalist ideals have guided the church for generations. As an institution, the Catholic Church has long opposed abortion, marriage of priests, the ordination of women as priests, contraception, and other liberal ideals.

> " Extremely orthodox Jews are members of a number of sects, such as the Hasidim, who are known for their conservative dress, beards, and long hair as well as their devotion to Jewish prayer, customs, dietary laws, and rituals. "

On the other hand, many Catholic leaders do not accept a literal interpretation of the Bible. In 1950 Pope Pius XII issued an encyclical, a letter explaining Catholic doctrine, in which he found no conflict between Darwin's explanation of evolution and Catholic beliefs. Forty-six years later, Pope John Paul II reinforced that notion, asserting that the strong scientific evidence supporting evolution could not be denied. Said John Paul, "Fresh knowledge leads to recognition of the theory of evolution as more than just a hypothesis."[12]

Other popes have tried to find ways to blend traditional Catholic beliefs with modern thinking. Shortly before he was elected Pope Benedict XVI in

2005, Cardinal Joseph Ratzinger suggested that fundamentalism has a place in modern Catholicism. Said Ratzinger, "Having a clear faith, based on the creed of the church, is often labeled today as fundamentalism."[13] In 2007 Benedict took a step toward a more fundamentalist approach to Catholicism when he urged Roman Catholic priests to speak Latin more often during mass.

Jewish Fundamentalism

Extremely orthodox Jews are members of a number of sects, such as the Hasidim, which are known for their conservative dress, beards, and long hair as well as their devotion to Jewish prayer, customs, dietary laws, and rituals. (*Hasid* is a Hebrew word that means "pious.") In America, Hasidic Jews have established many communities, one of the largest of which is in the Crown Heights neighborhood of Brooklyn, New York.

About 180,000 Hasidic Jews are believed to be living in America, composing a small fraction of America's 5 million Jews. (Jewish leaders acknowledge the difficulty in estimating the Hasidic population because Hasidic Jews do not generally talk to outsiders or answer their questions, which means they do not respond to polls.)

Since Jewish fundamentalists are represented in such small numbers in American Jewish society, it would appear their influence on American Jewish life is minimal. According to a study by the Center for Jewish Studies at City University of New York, the fastest growing movement within American Judaism between 1990 and 2000 was the Reform movement, which is regarded as among the most liberal of Jewish ideologies. The center's study found that in 2000, some 41 percent of American Jews who belong to synagogues attend Reform services, up from 35 percent in 1990.

Fundamentalist Jews are also in the minority in Israel, where they compose about 13 percent of the Jewish population of 5.3 million. But

> " In India, about 4.5 million members compose the fundamentalist Hindu movement known as Rashtriya Swayamsevak Sangh. The group's aim is to achieve 'Hindu supremacy,' meaning they wish to rid India of non-Hindu faiths, particularly Islam. "

unlike in the United States, fundamentalist Jews in Israel influence both lifestyle and politics. In Israel fundamentalist Jews have formed political parties and often participate in conservative blocs that hold considerable influence over the actions of the Israeli parliament.

Hindu Fundamentalism

In India about 4.5 million people are members of the fundamentalist Hindu movement known as Rashtriya Swayamsevak Sangh (RSS). The group's aim is to achieve "Hindu supremacy," meaning they wish to rid India of non-Hindu faiths, particularly Islam. (In English, the name of the RSS translates into the rather innocent-sounding "National Volunteers Association.") In a country of more than 1.1 billion people, the RSS remains a minority movement. Nevertheless, the group's influence has been growing, particularly in the Indian state of Gujarat. In Gujarat, RSS followers have won 117 seats in the 182-seat state assembly.

> Dawkins is particularly hostile toward scientists who he believes skew the results of their work to conform with fundamentalist notions about the origins of life. Some scientists have contributed to theories that try to merge religious principles with evolutionary science.

Fundamentalist Hindus adhere to strict religious practices such as fasting and making pilgrimages to holy shrines. They also actively encourage the replacement of mosques with Hindu shrines. Violence has often broken out in Gujarat, usually prompted by fundamentalist RSS leaders.

And the Hindu fundamentalist movement appears to be spreading elsewhere in India. "The threat of Islamic terror in India is rising," said Hindu fundamentalist leader Bal Thackeray, who heads the group Shiv Sena, based in the city of Mumbai. "It is time to counter the same with Hindu terror. Hindu suicide squads should be readied to ensure the existence of Hindu society and to protect the nation."[14]

In 2008, months after Thackeray leveled that threat, teams of Islamic terrorists based in Pakistan slipped into Mumbai and attacked hotels and a Jewish community center, where they took 171 lives. In Mumbai as well as other Indian cities, anger between Hindu and Islamic fundamentalists continues to be a major concern.

The New Atheists

As fundamentalists exert their influence, a vocal group of atheists has grown in influence, contending that fundamentalism prohibits the expansion of science and, ultimately, the growth of society. According to the Pew Forum, 1.6 percent of Americans—about 5 million people—regard themselves as atheists.

British biologist Richard Dawkins, author of *The God Delusion,* has emerged as a leader of the so-called New Atheist movement. "As a scientist, I am hostile to fundamentalist religion because it actively debauches the scientific enterprise," says Dawkins. "It teaches us not to change our minds, and not to want to know exciting things that are available to be known. It subverts science and saps intellect."[15]

Dawkins is particularly hostile toward scientists whom he believes skew the results of their work to conform with fundamentalist notions about the origins of life. Some scientists have contributed to theories that try to merge religious principles with evolutionary science, developing the notions of flood geology, which suggests the Great Flood is supported by geological evidence; theistic evolution, which maintains that evolution is guided by a divine plan; and intelligent design, which holds that life is too complicated to have evolved on its own, and therefore the evolution of people and other forms of life was helped by another entity—an "intelligent designer." "Fundamentalist religion is hell-bent on ruining the scientific education of countless thousands of innocent, well-meaning, eager young minds,"[16] insists Dawkins.

As fundamentalists try to establish themselves within the greater society, they often clash with people who feel that religious and moral ideals should be confined to the home and church. Fundamentalists are often in disagreement with people whose spiritual beliefs may be more liberal and accepting of change. Despite the influence of fundamentalists over American Protestantism or, in the Middle East, over Islam, in the context of world society as a whole most people do not regard themselves as fundamentalists. In most places fundamentalists have always been, and will always be, in the minority—a role that many fundamentalists have often been unwilling to accept.

How Widespread Is Religious Fundamentalism?

66 Fundamentalism, which stresses strict and literal adherence to a set of basic principles, is worrisome in any form, whether it be social, political or religious. Religious fundamentalists, however, are particularly dangerous. In attempting to impose their views on the rest of the world, religious fundamentalists are hostile to anything that disagrees with their religion. 99

—John W. Whitehead, "The Worldwide Danger of Religious Fundamentalism,"
Huffington Post, December 19, 2008. www.huffingtonpost.com.

Whitehead is a constitutional attorney and founder of the Rutherford Institute in Charlottesville, Virginia, which studies civil liberties issues.

66 My fundamentalist education gave me a profound respect for my fellow human beings; it taught me the dangers of pride and the joys of helping others; it gave me a love of the Bible and a lifelong devotion to language and music. 99

—Christine Rosen, *My Fundamentalist Education: A Memoir of a Divine Girlhood.* New York: Public Affairs, 2005.

Rosen is senior editor of the *New Atlantis* and a fellow of the Ethics and Public Policy Center, Washington, D.C.

Bracketed quotes indicate conflicting positions.

* Editor's Note: While the definition of a primary source can be narrowly or broadly defined, for the purposes of Compact Research, a primary source consists of: 1) results of original research presented by an organization or researcher; 2) eyewitness accounts of events, personal experience, or work experience; 3) first-person editorials offering pundits' opinions; 4) government officials presenting political plans and/or policies; 5) representatives of organizations presenting testimony or policy.

66 **Whether political or religious, of local or global scope, fundamentalism is a phenomenon to be seriously reckoned with.** 99

> —Douglas Pratt, "Terrorism and Religious Fundamentalism: Prospects for a Predictive Paradigm," *Marburg Journal of Religion,* June 2006.

Pratt is associate professor of philosophy and religious studies, University of Waikato, New Zealand.

66 **Today, religious fundamentalism has penetrated all major religions, the most obvious being Islam, and has become a dangerous, worldwide phenomenon. It is essentially a reaction, at times violent, against most things 'modern,' including democracy.** 99

> —Bert B. Beach, "Religious Freedom or Religious Fundamentalism?" *Liberty Magazine,* December 30, 2007. http://shadow.libertymagazine.org.

Beach is secretary-general emeritus of the International Religious Liberty Association in Silver Spring, Maryland.

66 **Muslim fundamentalists believe that everyday survival is a sufficient reason to establish a political system of a state that is based on God's teachings because they view existing Western powers as unjust. The best solution, they believe, is to rise up against Western powers with the aim to fight oppression, exploitation, tyranny and the unjust political manifestations.** 99

> —Nadwa Arar, "In Defense of Radical Behavior: Is Muslim Fundamentalism a Threat to the West?" *Middle East Times,* October 7, 2008. www.metimes.com.

Arar is a novelist, journalist, and graduate of the School of Oriental and African Studies at London University in Great Britain.

❝I think many of us—I just do not mean trained theologians, but ordinary folks in churches, mosques and synagogues as well—have found ways to be religious without being either stupid or homicidal.❞

—William C. Placher, "Fighting Atheist," *Christian Century,* September 18, 2007.

Placher is a professor of religion and philosophy at Wabash College in Indiana and author of the book *The Triune God: An Essay in Postliberal Theology.*

❝Fundamentalism points us to the important task that confronts the church in every generation, namely, the vigorous assertion without compromise of such key truths as the Trinity, the deity of the lord Jesus Christ, his bodily incarnation and resurrection from the dead. The passion for the truth gripped the early fundamentalists and it needs to grip us as well.❞

—Michael Haykin, "A Pastors' and Theologians' Forum on Fundamentalism," *The 9 Marks,* March/April 2008. www.9marks.org.

Haykin is professor of church history and biblical spirituality at Southern Baptist Theological Seminary, Louisville, Kentucky.

❝The first and most basic distinguishing feature of fundamentalist movements is that they are reactive. Fundamentalists believe that their religion is under mortal threat from the secularism of the modern world, and they are fighting back. They may resist in different ways, but they are essentially oppositional; they have to have an enemy.❞

—Peter Herriot, *Religious Fundamentalism: Global, Local and Personal.* London: Routledge, 2009.

Herriot is an author and retired professor at the University of Surrey in Great Britain.

---

66 Religious hatreds are easy to inflate and exploit. There is plenty of free-floating unhappiness just waiting to be channeled, and Hindu fundamentalists are brilliant at creating issues where none exists. 99

—Jo McGowan, "Pious Carnage," *Commonweal*, January 31, 2008.

McGowan is an American author who lives in India.

Facts and Illustrations

How Widespread Is Religious Fundamentalism?

- About 15 million Catholics, or about **23 percent** of the Catholic population in America, believe in the literal meaning of the Bible.

- **31 percent** of Americans—about 95 million people—believe the Bible word for word, according to a 2007 poll by the Gallup Organization.

- The 10 largest megachurches in America all espouse the belief that the Bible is unerring; they have a combined membership of more than **220,000 worshippers**.

- **62 percent** of worshippers in black churches regard themselves as fundamentalists; most are members of Methodist, Baptist, and Pentecostal traditions.

- The fundamentalist Seventh-Day Adventist Church, which observes the belief that the heavens and the Earth were created by God in six days, includes an international membership of some **15 million** people.

- According to Amnesty International, at least 3 people convicted of violations of sharia law in Iran have been **stoned to death** since 2002; by 2008 another 9 people were convicted and awaiting their penalties to be carried out.

- Evidence that fundamentalist Islam is growing in Turkey, a country with a secular government, can be found in recent elections: In 2007 the fundamentalist Justice and Development Party won **47 percent** of the vote; in 2002 the party won **34 percent** of the vote.

Religions in America

Christians make up nearly 80 percent of the population of the United States. Most are Protestants, about half of whom belong to evangelical churches. Fundamentalists make up the majorities at the evangelical churches, but they also belong to other Protestant traditions as well as the Catholic Church and non-Christian faiths, including Judaism, Islam, and Hinduism.

Other World Religions **0.3%**
Hindu **0.4%**
Muslim **0.6%**
Other Faiths **1.2%**
Buddhist **0.7%**
Jewish **1.7%**
Other Christian **0.3%**
Orthodox **0.6%**
Jehovah's Witnesses **0.7%**
Mormon **1.7%**

Unaffiliated **16.1%**
Evangelical (Protestant) **26.3%**
Catholic **23.9%**
Mainline Churches (Protestant) **18.1%**
Don't know/refused **0.8%**
African American Churches (Protestant) **6.9%**

Note: due to rounding totals do not add to 100 percent.

Source: Pew Forum on Religion and Public Life, "U.S. Religious Landscape Survey," February 2008. http://religions.pewforum.org.

Fundamentalists Believe in the Literal Interpretation of Texts

Fundamentalists believe in a literal interpretation of the scriptures, meaning they believe the Bible, the Qur'an or other holy texts word for word. A poll found that evangelical Christians, members of African American churches, Jehovah's Witnesses, and Muslims are most likely to adopt fundamentalist interpretations of their scriptures.

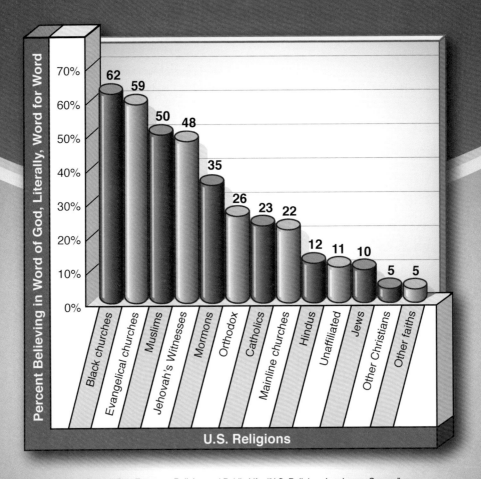

Source: Pew Forum on Religion and Public Life, "U.S. Religious Landscape Survey," February 2008. http://religions.pewforum.org.

• A 2008 survey of Muslims in Indonesia found **52 percent** favoring establishment of an Islamic-based legal code and **40 percent** believing the penalty for theft should include cutting off the hands of thieves.

The 10 Largest Megachurches

There are more than 900 megachurches in the United States, each delivering services to 2,000 or more worshippers. The 10 largest megachurches all preach fundamentalist Christian messages. The largest of the megachurches is Lakewood Church in Houston, Texas, which had to take over a former NBA arena to accommodate worshippers.

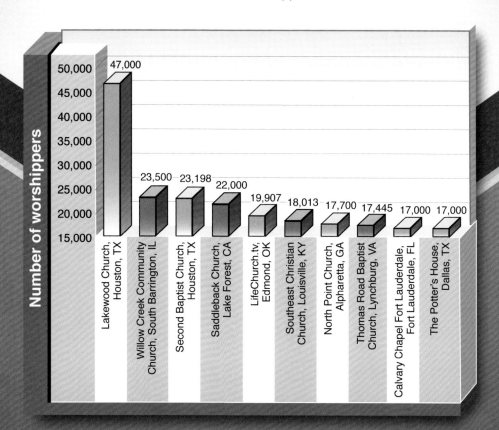

Source: Outreach, "100 Largest and Fastest-Growing U.S. Churches," 2007. www.outreachmagazine.com.

Mixed Support for Sharia Law in Iran

Sharia, which means "the path," is the law that governs Islamic life, guiding how Muslims eat, dress, worship, and conduct themselves in relationships with others. Some countries, including Iran, have adopted a fundamentalist approach to the sharia and have instituted such harsh penalties as stoning for adultery. A poll of Iranian citizens found, however, that just 14 percent believe sharia should be the only source of the country's laws, indicating a resistance to the regime's fundamentalist approach to the government. A large majority believe sharia should have some influence on the country's law.

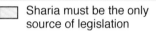 Sharia must be the only source of legislation

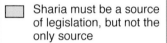 Sharia must be a source of legislation, but not the only source

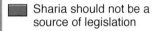 Sharia should not be a source of legislation

 Don't know/Refused

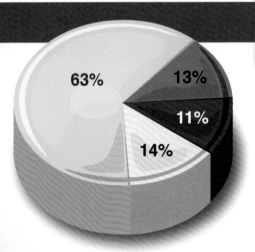

63%   13%   11%   14%

Note: Total exceeds 100 due to rounding.

Source: Magali Rheault and Dalia Mogahed, "Iranians, Egyptians, Turks: Contrasting Views on *Sharia*," Gallup Organization, July 10, 2008. www.gallup.com.

- In India the Hindu fundamentalist movement Rashtriya Swayamse-vak Sangh includes about **4.5 million** members, most of whom live in the state of Gujarat.

Does Religious Fundamentalism Threaten Individual Rights?

66 The majority of women I know like wearing the hijab, which leaves the face uncovered. . . . It is a personal statement: My dress tells you I am a Muslim and I expect to be treated respectfully. 99

—Yvonne Ridley, British journalist who converted to Islam after visiting Afghanistan.

66 The belief of a woman who does not want to wear a veil must be respected. This is the essence of democracy, in my opinion, to respect and accept the opinion of the other. 99

—Nouriya al-Subeeh, the minister of education for Kuwait who has rejected a requirement under sharia law to wear a veil in public.

After years of occupation by the Soviet Union followed by a civil war, the fundamentalist Islamic regime that called itself the Taliban seized power in Afghanistan. In the Pashto language, which is spoken in Afghanistan, the term *Taliban* means "students of Islamic knowledge." The leader of the movement, Mohammed Omar, is a mullah, a term for a Muslim who is learned in Islamic law.

After taking power, the Taliban instituted a strict interpretation of sharia law throughout the country. Soon, Afghans found their human rights severely curtailed: Women were forced to dress in the burka, a head-to-toe garment covering all but their eyes; gays, prostitutes, and adulterers were publicly executed, often by stoning; thieves lost their hands on the chopping block; and others were imprisoned for minor infractions of sharia. Even the growing of beards was covered under sharia law—all adult Afghan men were ordered to stop shaving.

The Taliban was ousted in October 2001 by an American-led military invasion in response to the September 11 attacks—the regime had sheltered terrorists from al Qaeda as they planned the strikes on the Pentagon and World Trade Center. The new government has relaxed some of the strictest measures of sharia law, but infractions are still punished harshly. The wearing of the burka, for example, is voluntary, but many women still observe Islamic law and custom by covering themselves completely when they are outdoors.

> " Afghans found their human rights severely curtailed: Women were forced to dress in the burka, a head-to-toe garment covering all but their eyes; gays, prostitutes, and adulterers were publicly executed, often by stoning; thieves lost their hands on the chopping block; and others were imprisoned for minor infractions of the sharia. "

In Afghanistan individuals often find their rights sacrificed as they comply with the fundamentalist brand of Islam that governs their society. People who live in other fundamentalist Islamic countries have also been denied rights guaranteed to others who live under more progressive regimes. In Saudi Arabia, for example, women are not permitted to vote or drive cars. In 1990 about 20 Saudi women defied the law against driving by operating their family cars in downtown Riyadh, the Saudi capital. They were arrested, taken into custody and released only when their husbands or other male relatives signed statements promising that the women would never drive again. Later, some lost their jobs and had their passports revoked. Moreover, leaflets circulated in Riyadh carrying their names and referring to them as whores. All those punishments were heaped on the women simply for driving the family cars.

Acceptance of the Hijab

Many women remain a part of their fundamentalist cultures, accepting their roles because they believe strongly in their religious principles. Even when they travel, they continue to observe fundamentalist laws that govern them at home.

People who attended the 2008 Summer Olympic Games in Beijing may have seen events featuring Ruqaya al Ghasara, a sprinter from Bahrain. While Al Ghasara's opponents in the women's track events competed in tank tops and shorts, Al Ghasara ran dressed in a head covering and full body suit that completely covered her torso, arms and legs.

The scarf worn by Al Ghasara is known as a *hijab*. It covers the head of a Muslim woman, including her hair. "I want to say I'm very thankful for being a Muslim; it's a blessing," said Al Ghasara. "Wearing a veil proves that Muslim women face no obstacles and encourages them to participate in sport. This is a glory to all Muslim women."[17]

Breaking Away from Tradition

In many fundamentalist societies, women are taught that their place is to raise the children and provide comfortable homes for their husbands. They are denied the opportunities to pursue educations or careers. Such circumstances are typical in a country like Saudi Arabia where the government has adopted fundamentalist religious principles as law.

In other places, though, it is not unusual for women and others to break away from fundamentalist traditions. In America women are guaranteed equal treatment under law. Some young Hasidic women have elected to take advantage of the opportunities available to them in America, even if it means breaking away from a culture they have known since their childhoods.

> Some young Hasidic women have elected to take advantage of the opportunities available to them in America, even if it means breaking away from a culture they have known since their childhoods.

In Crown Heights, Malkie Schwartz is the oldest of nine children born to devout parents who are members of a Hasidic sect known as the Lubavitchers. After high school, she hoped to join a Lubavitcher group known as *schluchim*, whose members work to spread fundamentalist Judaism to other Jews. To prepare for her role within the *schluchim,* Schwartz spent a year in Israel at a fundamentalist seminary. Instead of committing herself more deeply to Jewish fundamentalism, though, her year in Israel away from the cloistered lifestyle of her home in Brooklyn opened her eyes to how other Jews live and how they take advantage of opportunities to improve their lives. Near the end of her year in Israel, she announced to her stunned family that she intended to go to college. "I felt I couldn't make this decision [to remain in Hasidism]," said Schwartz. "I wanted an education."[18]

> "In places where governments rule by democratic principles, cultures often clash when fundamentalists believe their way of life has been endangered by what are otherwise regarded as basic freedoms."

She returned home, moved in with her grandmother and enrolled in Hunter College in New York. Now, instead of wearing the long conservative dresses familiar in the Hasidic community, Schwartz dresses in T-shirts and jeans. Instead of preparing for marriage, she studied philosophy and earned her degree. Following college, Schwartz founded Footsteps, a group that helps other young Jews find their ways in society after leaving the cloistered worlds of their Hasidic homes. The group helps former Hasidic Jews obtain their general equivalency diplomas, learn social networking skills, and find educational opportunities. Since its inception, more than 200 former Hasidic Jews, including women and men, have sought counseling from Footsteps.

Cultures Clash over Free Speech

In countries like Saudi Arabia and Afghanistan, the government is guided by fundamentalist principles: Anybody who does not go along risks the wrath of the law. In places where governments rule by democratic principles, cultures often clash when fundamentalists believe their way of life has been endangered by what are otherwise regarded as basic freedoms. Sometimes the culture clash can turn violent.

In 2004 a film titled *Submission* aired on Dutch TV. Directed by Theo van Gogh, a descendant of painter Vincent van Gogh, the film chronicled the mistreatment of women in Islamic cultures. In one scene, the camera focuses on words from the Qur'an inscribed on a woman's body over welt marks, evidently caused by a whip. Clearly, Van Gogh intended to convey the message that women are abused under fundamentalist interpretations of sharia law.

Van Gogh committed no crime—the constitution of the Netherlands supports freedom of expression. Still, more than a million Muslims live in the Netherlands, and many seethed at what they perceived as anti-Islamic messages and images depicted in *Submission.* In the mosques of Amsterdam, the imams—the Islamic scholars who lead religious services—railed against the film. One worshipper who heard those complaints was Mohammed Bouyeri, a Moroccan who had embraced fundamentalist Islam and joined a Dutch terror cell.

Two months after the film aired on Dutch TV, Bouyeri confronted Van Gogh on an Amsterdam street, shot him six times, then slit his throat. Finally, he pinned a note to Van Gogh's chest proclaiming the filmmaker's murder a triumph for Islam. Although Van Gogh was within his rights under Dutch law to produce and air the film, to Bouyeri and other fundamentalist Muslims living in the Netherlands he had committed a crime against Islam. They believed the fundamentalist principles of sharia and the Qur'an outweighed the laws of their host country. A year after Van Gogh's death, Bouyeri stood trial for the murder. He admitted to the crime and showed no remorse, contending Van Gogh was an enemy of Islam. "I acted out of conviction and not out of hate," Bouyeri said. "If I'm ever released, I'd do the same again. Exactly the same."[19]

Two years after Van Gogh's murder, radical Muslims again railed against the criticisms of Islam that were published in a society that values freedom of expression. In nearby Denmark, rioting erupted after the newspaper *Jyllands-Posten* published a dozen cartoons depicting the prophet Muhammad, infuriating

> " Angry Muslims staged demonstrations in which they burned the Danish flag, demanded the ouster of the Danish ambassadors from Islamic countries, and threatened to kill the 12 cartoonists who drew the images. "

Islamic fundamentalists. Many Muslims consider it sacrilegious to depict a likeness of Muhammad. Lampooning the prophet further angered them—among the most incendiary of the cartoons was a depiction of Muhammad with a bomb in his turban.

Soon, the rioting spread throughout Europe and the Middle East. Angry Muslims staged demonstrations in which they burned the Danish flag, demanded the ouster of the Danish ambassadors from Islamic countries, and threatened to kill the 12 cartoonists who drew the images. Tempers eventually eased after *Jyllands-Posten* as well as the Danish government issued apologies.

As in the Netherlands, the Danish constitution supports freedom of expression—*Jyllands-Posten* broke no laws by publishing the cartoons—but the rioting and death threats served to stifle the rights of the cartoonists to express themselves as well as the right of a free press to publish their work. Meanwhile, since the cartoons were first published, many of the artists have remained in hiding. Those who continue to work said they have no intention of producing cartoons again that would provoke anger among Muslims—proof, they acknowledged, that the Islamic fundamentalists succeeded in stifling their rights to free speech.

> **When the votes were totaled and the fundamentalist Christian leaders were able to proclaim victory, gays contended that the fundamentalists had used their influence to deny what should be universal rights to a small and oppressed minority.**

Overreaching on Abortion

In many societies fundamentalists have attempted to use the democratic process to change the law, making it conform more closely to their views and principles. In some cases fundamentalists have proven themselves to be dedicated and effective campaigners, capable of swaying majorities of the electorate to their way of thinking. Left in their wake, though, are the people in the minority whose rights may be sacrificed because they oppose the fundamentalist position.

In other cases, efforts by fundamentalists to sway public opinion have fallen short. Often, they have overreached—trying for too radical a change in a society where people prefer to live under more moderate principles.

In 2008 fundamentalist Christians in California campaigned in favor of a ban on same-sex marriages slated as a referendum on the election day ballot. The fundamentalists were able to call on tremendous organizational and fund-raising reserves to help convince mainstream voters of their positions and outlaw same-sex marriages. When the votes were totaled and the fundamentalist Christian leaders were able to proclaim victory, gays contended that the fundamentalists had used their influence to deny what should be universal rights to a small and oppressed minority.

Fundamentalist Christians are also vehemently antiabortion and, as with their opposition to gay marriage, have often used their political influence to enact strict antiabortion state laws. However, some states have rejected fundamentalist campaigns and the strict antiabortion laws they promote.

During the 2008 election fundamentalists campaigned in favor of a South Dakota law banning virtually all abortions, but it was rejected by voters. In Colorado voters rejected a measure establishing human life at the moment of conception—a concept backed by antiabortion activists. And in California voters rejected a ballot initiative that would have required parents to receive 48 hours notice before daughters under the age of 18 could receive abortions. Following the campaign, observers suggested the fundamentalists attempted to enact too many restrictions on individual rights that affected too many people. Unlike the same-sex marriage ban, the curtailments of abortion rights had the potential to affect households throughout the three states.

Experts suggested that the fundamentalists would have done well to seek compromises with their opponents—changes in their states' abortion

> **Following the campaign, observers suggested the fundamentalists overreached—that they attempted to enact too many restrictions on individual rights that affected too many people.**

laws where both sides felt changes may be needed. "Where the movement has been most successful is when they have adopted consensus positions," said George Mason University professor Mark Rozell, an expert on Christian conservatives. "When they move beyond consensus positions, it's a tough battle."[20]

Certainly, as the 2008 election day results show, fundamentalists in America do not enjoy free rein to exert their principles on others—voters in three states rejected restrictions on abortion. Elsewhere in the world, the rights of individuals have often been endangered by fundamentalist movements. Under the oppressive Taliban regime, the rights of women were clearly abused. In the Netherlands a prominent filmmaker was murdered because his support for the rights of Islamic women was regarded by some fundamentalist Muslims as an insult to Islam. And in Denmark the cartoonists whose only crime was to use their art to render images of a religious icon have been forced into hiding, their freedom of speech curtailed while their lives remain very much in jeopardy.

Does Religious Fundamentalism Threaten Individual Rights?

"In this sharia society, women are subordinate to men. They must be confined to their houses, beaten if found disobedient, forced into marriage, and hidden behind the veil. The hands of thieves are cut off and capital punishment is performed on crowded public squares in front of cheering crowds."

—Ayaan Hirsi Ali, *The Caged Virgin: An Emancipation Proclamation for Women and Islam.* New York: Free Press, 2008.

Ali, a native of Somalia, is a former member of the Dutch parliament. She is a writer and was coproducer with Theo van Gogh of the film *Submission*.

"Jordan's constitutional freedom of religion expresses core Arab-Islamic values—a calling to peace; respect for others; the commandment to social justice. This is the voice of Islam as it has been taught and practiced for over a thousand years, and it is the opposite of the ignorant ideology of hate shouted by today's extremist elements."

—King Abdullah II, "Clash of Civilizations and Extremists," September 12, 2005. www.kingabdullah.jo.

Abdullah II, the king of Jordan, maintains strong ties to the West and is regarded as a moderating influence in the Middle East.

* Editor's Note: While the definition of a primary source can be narrowly or broadly defined, for the purposes of Compact Research, a primary source consists of: 1) results of original research presented by an organization or researcher; 2) eyewitness accounts of events, personal experience, or work experience; 3) first-person editorials offering pundits' opinions; 4) government officials presenting political plans and/or policies; 5) representatives of organizations presenting testimony or policy.

Primary Source Quotes

66 The question of individual rights occupies a smaller place in Islam than in Western . . . thought. Self-determination, the most crucial guarantee sanctioned by natural law, is explicitly denied in Islam: not the human being is sovereign, but God. 99

—Peter R. Demant, *Islam vs. Islamism: The Dilemma of the Modern World.* Westport, CT: Praeger, 2006.

Demant is a professor of history at Universidade de Saõ Paulo, Brazil, where he lectures in international relations and contemporary Asian history.

66 Among the dozens of limitations on religious freedom in the Arab-Islamic world are the crimes of apostasy—converting from Islam to another religion—and blasphemy against the prophet Muhammad, both punishable by death under Muslim sharia law. Coptic Christians are, at best, second-class citizens in Egypt; Baha'is are savagely persecuted in Iran; and churches and synagogues are banned in Saudi Arabia, as is any non-Muslim religious activity in public. 99

—Rick Santorum, "Intimidating Critics of Islam," *Philadelphia Inquirer,* February 12, 2009.

Santorum is a former U.S. senator from Pennsylvania.

66 I cannot help but glimpse the spirit of the Holy Qur'an's message on pluralism in the lines that [Dr. Martin Luther] King uttered at the end of the Montgomery bus boycott: 'We have before us the glorious opportunity to inject a new dimension of love into the veins of our civilization.' 99

—Eboo Patel, *Acts of Faith.* Boston: Beacon, 2007.

Patel is an author and Islamic scholar who heads Interfaith Youth Core, a Chicago-based group that enlists young people of different faiths for public service projects.

"Women and social minorities are increasingly the victims of fundamentalist forces fighting in the name of the traditional family and morality and against the sexual permissiveness represented supposedly by adolescent sexuality, homosexuality, non-traditional families, and the AIDS epidemic."

—Asoka Banderage, "Fundamentalism and Women's Rights," Committee on Women, Population, and the Environment, July 20, 2006. http://cwpe.org.

Banderage is associate professor of women's studies at Mount Holyoke College in South Hadley, Massachusetts.

"Fundamentalists demonstrate two valuable lessons to other followers of Jesus. On the one hand, they rebuke us for our lack of courage. Each of us must be prepared to take up our cross and count the cost. On the other hand, they warn us of the unintended consequences of faith in a fallen world."

—Os Guinness, "A Pastors' and Theologians' Forum on Fundamentalism," *The 9 Marks,* March/April 2008. www.9marks.org.

Guinness is a theologian and founder of Washington, D.C.–based Trinity Forum, which studies the impact of religion on society.

"Although no group has profited more from the First Amendment and the disestablishment of religion in America than evangelicals, the Religious Right would love nothing more than to dismantle the First Amendment and enshrine evangelical values and mores as the law of the land."

—Randall Balmer, *Thy Kingdom Come: An Evangelical's Lament.* New York: Basic Books, 2006.

Balmer is professor of American religious history at Barnard College, Columbia University, and a visiting professor at Yale University Divinity School.

66 The affair between fundamentalism and homophobia has been a long and faithful one. What's new and chilling, however, is the single-minded ideological obsession of it. 99

—Michelle Goldberg, "The Sexual Threat of Fundamentalism," *Religion Dispatches,* December 29, 2008. www.religiondispatches.org.

Goldberg is the author of *Kingdom Coming: The Rise of Christian Nationalism.*

66 Anyone who has been watching the Christian right chip away at abortion access and the separation of church and state knows that criminalizing abortion is just the tip of the Christian-fundamentalist iceberg and that their agenda is global in scope. 99

—Yifat Susskind, "It's Not Just an Abortion Ban: The Christian Right's Global Agenda," Association for Women's Rights in Development, December 2, 2008. www.awid.org.

Susskind is communications director for MADRE, a New York–based women's rights group.

Does Religious Fundamentalism Threaten Individual Rights?

- Wealthy Muslims have offered rewards as high as **$1 million** to the Muslim who kills Kurt Westergaard, the Danish cartoonist who was driven into hiding after depicting the prophet Muhammad with a bomb in his turban.

- A poll found that **57 percent** of Danes supported the decision by the newspaper *Jyllands-Posten* to publish the 12 cartoons lampooning the prophet Muhammad.

- Women are not allowed to vote or run for public office in Saudi Arabia; it is the only country in the Islamic world in which **women are barred from participating in the political process**.

- In Kuwait, women have been allowed to vote and hold political office since 2005; by 2008 no women had been elected to parliament, while Islamic fundamentalists, who oppose rights for women, held **21 of the parliament's 50 seats**.

- **84 percent** of voters who are members of evangelical Christian churches supported Proposition 8, a measure that made same-sex marriage illegal in California.

- Four years after the ouster of the Taliban, **90 percent** of Afghan citizens surveyed say they support education for girls, **89 percent** said women should have the right to vote, **75 percent** support employment opportunities for women, and **66 percent** said women should hold public office.

Few in Afghanistan Favor a Return of the Taliban

Although Taliban fighters continue to wage a guerilla war in Afghanistan, few citizens of Aghanistan favor a return of the fundamentalist Islamic regime to power. Just 5 percent of Afghan citizens supported the presence of Taliban fighters in their country, while 11 percent supported the presence of foreign jihadists. Meanwhile, attitudes about the treatment of women have grown much more liberal in Afghanistan since the days when women were forced to wear burkas and often whipped or beaten in public. Many Afghan citizens oppose hitting or beating women, but there is still support for arranged marriages, and many citizens of the country find it unacceptable for women to hold supervisory jobs over men.

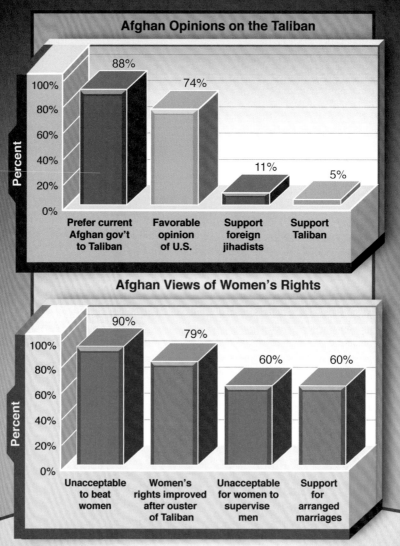

Source: Gary Langer, "2006 Poll: Strife Erodes Afghan Optimism," ABC News, December 7, 2006. http://abcnews.com.

Does Religious Fundamentalism Threaten Individual Rights?

Mixed Results on Social Issues

In California, voters adopted a ballot initiative in 2008 to ban same-sex marriages, in large part due to the efforts of fundamentalist Christians as well as conservative Mormons. Elsewhere, however, fundamentalists were disappointed by the results of the 2008 elections as voters rejected limits on abortions in California and South Dakota. In Colorado, voters rejected the antiabortion position that would have defined life as beginning at the moment of conception.

South Dakota Abortion Referendum

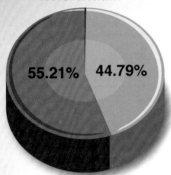

55.21% 44.79%

A "yes" vote outlawed abortion except in cases of rape or incest or a danger to the mother's health.

California Abortion Referendum

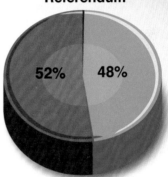

52% 48%

A "yes" vote favored notification of parents before a minor's abortion.

California Same-Sex Marriage

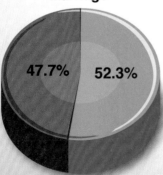

47.7% 52.3%

A "yes" vote favored elimination of same-sex marriage.

Colorado Abortion Referendum

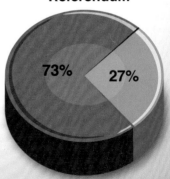

73% 27%

A "yes" vote defined human life at the moment of conception.

No   Yes

Sources: Office of the South Dakota secretary of state, 2008. www.sdsos.gov; Office of the California secretary of state, 2008. http://vote.sos.ca.gov; My Fox Colorado, "Colorado Election Results," 2008. http://media/myfoxcolorado.com.

Women Are Not Treated as Equals in the Islamic World

In America, anyone who is old enough can vote or drive, but in the Islamic world that is not necessarily the case. In Saudi Arabia, the country's fundamentalist interpretation of the sharia prohibits women from voting or operating cars. Women often share in the belief that they do not qualify for equal rights. In Saudi Arabia, 69 percent of women think they should have the right to vote, while 61 percent feel they should have the right to drive automobiles. In other Islamic countries, acceptance of women's rights is hardly unanimous among men and women.

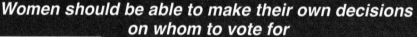

Women should be able to make their own decisions on whom to vote for

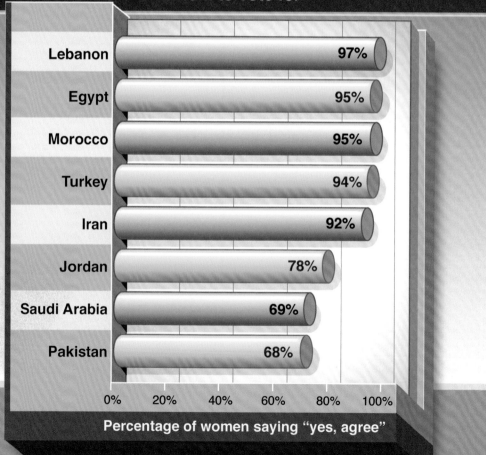

Country	Percentage
Lebanon	97%
Egypt	95%
Morocco	95%
Turkey	94%
Iran	92%
Jordan	78%
Saudi Arabia	69%
Pakistan	68%

Percentage of women saying "yes, agree"

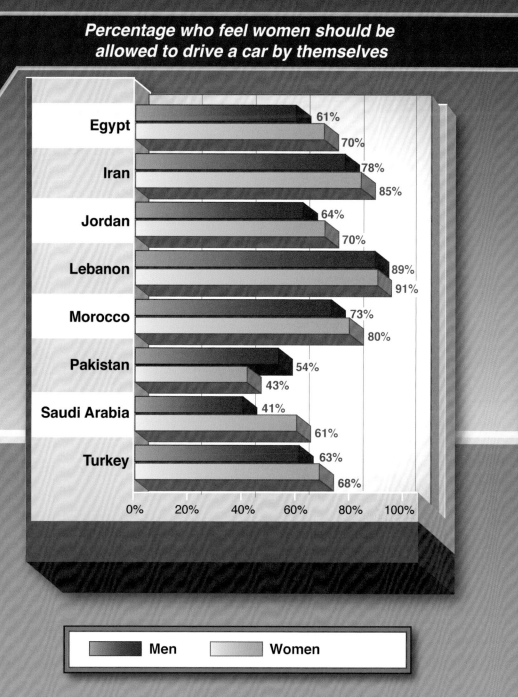

Percentage who feel women should be allowed to drive a car by themselves

Country	Men	Women
Egypt	61%	70%
Iran	78%	85%
Jordan	64%	70%
Lebanon	89%	91%
Morocco	73%	80%
Pakistan	54%	43%
Saudi Arabia	41%	61%
Turkey	63%	68%

Men   Women

Source: Gallup Organization, "Perspectives of Women in the Muslim World," February 15, 2008. www.galluppoll.com.

53

- Homosexuality is illegal in Saudi Arabia; according to the United Nations Refugee Agency, at least **120 gay men have been arrested** in the kingdom since 2005. They have received sentences of up to 2 years in prison as well as 2,000 lashes.

- A 2008 Gallup Organization poll found that **56 percent** of Americans agree with the fundamentalist Christian position that same-sex marriage should not be legal.

Does Religious Fundamentalism Fuel Violence and Terrorism?

> **The killing of those (who offend) is a matter that Allah likes, and that his prophet likes, Allah has ordered it and his prophet has incited for it.**
>
> —Osama bin Laden, head of al Qaeda and sponsor of the September 11, 2001, terrorist attacks in New York, Washington, D.C., and Pennsylvania.

> **Islam, as practiced by the vast majority of people, is a peaceful religion, a religion that respects others. Ours is a country based upon tolerance and we welcome people of all faiths in America.**
>
> —George W. Bush, forty-third president of the United States.

Since the bombing of the *Cole*, a navy destroyer that was attacked by a suicide bomber on October 12, 2000, Islamic extremism has been recognized as a worldwide threat. A year after the incident, extremists recruited by the al Qaeda network hijacked airliners, slamming them into the World Trade Center and Pentagon. The final death toll that day totaled more than 3,000.

The attacks of September 11, 2001, would not be the last time Islamic fundamentalists resorted to violence. According to the U.S. National Counterterrorism Center, each year about 14,000 acts of terrorism are committed across the globe, with the vast majority attributed to the actions of Islamic extremists. In 2007 about 67,000 people lost their lives in terrorist attacks; more than half the victims were Muslims.

Many of those acts of terrorism have occurred in Iraq where the United States has maintained a military presence following the 2003 invasion and ouster of dictator Saddam Hussein. Islamic fundamentalists do not want Americans on Muslim land and have often resorted to violent means to make their intentions clear. Not all of the attacks have been aimed at American soldiers—according to the National Counterterrorism Center, about 70 percent of the victims are civilians. Many extremists hope to drive the United States out of Iraq by keeping the violence level high and destabilizing the country.

> " Since the fall of the Soviet Union, Chechen extremists have fought sporadically with the Russian government, demanding independence so they can form a fundamentalist Islamic republic. "

In 2007 about 13,600 victims lost their lives in terrorist attacks in Iraq. Other countries that experienced high numbers of fatalities due to terrorism in 2007 included Afghanistan, where the United States and its allies are fighting against extremists of the former Taliban regime; Pakistan, which has long been a center of Islamic extremism; and India, where Hindu and Muslim extremists often clash. Death tolls in those countries in 2007 included about 2,000 in Afghanistan, 1,300 in Pakistan, and 1,100 in India.

In Russia about 150 victims lost their lives due to terrorist attacks. Many of those incidents have occurred in an Islam-dominated region of Russia known as Chechnya. Since the fall of the Soviet Union, Chechen extremists have fought sporadically with the Russian government, demanding independence so they can form a fundamentalist Islamic republic.

Sometimes violence spills out of Chechnya, afflicting other parts of Russia. One of the most horrific attacks by Islamic fundamentalists in recent years occurred in 2004 in North Ossetia, a region of the Russian Federation where Islamic extremists laid siege to a school, taking more than 1,200 people hostage. Most of the hostages were children. After a 3-day standoff, Russian commandos stormed the school. During the fighting, more than 300 people died, including nearly 200 children. The extremists who took the hostages were members of a terrorist cell known as the Islamic Brigade of Shahids, which has its roots in Chechnya.

The group draws its name from the word *shahid,* an Arabic term for "martyr." In the fundamentalist Islamic world, martyrs are willing to give their lives, often through suicide missions, to defeat the enemies of Islam. They willingly give their own lives in the belief that their sacrifices will be rewarded in heaven.

What Is Jihad?

Nearly 15 centuries ago, the prophet Muhammad counseled his followers against using the sword to spread Islam. "Let there be no violence in religion," declared the prophet. "If they embrace Islam they are surely directed; but if they turn their backs, verily to thee belongs preaching only."[21]

But Muhammad also raised the concept *of jihad,* an Arabic term that means "holy struggle," in the course of a war against a hostile Arab tribe that held to pagan beliefs. Said the prophet, "Allah loveth those who battle for his cause."[22]

Over the years, Islamic scholars have debated the meaning of Muhammad's words. Islamic fundamentalists have interpreted a passage in the Qur'an that includes the phrase *jihad fi sabil illah* to mean warfare against enemies of the Muslim community. Said Osama bin Laden, the founder and chief financier of al Qaeda, "Jihad today is a duty of every Muslim."[23]

Many Islamic scholars argue, though, that radicals have misinterpreted the meaning of jihad. They contend that the prophet Muhammad intended jihad to be an inner struggle in which Muslims strive to resist sin. They also contend that Islam is a pacifist faith and that Allah abhors violence.

> " In the 1980s Bin Laden answered the call for Muslims to participate in the war against the Soviet occupation of Afghanistan, volunteering for the mujahideen, or fighters in the jihad. "

What Motivates Islamic Terrorism?

The symbol of international Islamic extremism remains Bin Laden, a fugitive Saudi millionaire and the mastermind of the 2001 terrorist strikes. As with most fundamentalists, Bin Laden is influenced by ideas that were hatched centuries ago.

Some 700 years ago, the Islamic scholar Ibn Taymiyya was among the first Muslims to embrace a literal translation of the Qur'an, calling on Muslims to wage jihad against their enemies. Those enemies could even include other Muslims, whose piety and adherence to Islam were found by Taymiyya to be less than absolute.

In the 1940s Taymiyya's ideals were embraced by Egyptian scholar Sayyid Qutb, who had studied in America and had been repulsed by Western culture, particularly the freedoms granted to women. Qutb had already embraced Islamic fundamentalism; the three years he spent in America convinced him that for Islam to survive, it had to adhere to its most fundamentalist form. He would go on to write a 30-volume commentary on the Qur'an, defending the most literal interpretation of the prophet Muhammad's words. To Qutb, there was no doubt about the meaning of "jihad": It stood for holy war against nonbelievers, including Muslims who embraced Western civilization—even leaders of Muslim nations who maintained friendly relations with the United States and its allies.

> **By taking lives and sending shock waves through the population, fundamentalists have been able to accomplish political change—although they may have to sacrifice their own lives or freedom for the cause.**

Exactly when Bin Laden fell under the influence of Qutb, Taymiyya, and other Islamic fundamentalists is unclear. (Qutb died in 1966, executed by Egyptian president Gamal Abdel Nasser who regarded him as a threat to his regime.) In the 1980s Bin Laden answered the call for Muslims to participate in the war against the Soviet occupation of Afghanistan, volunteering for the mujahideen, or fighters in the jihad. Bin Laden rose in the mujahideen ranks; by the time the Soviets withdrew in 1989 he commanded his own mujahideen militia. One of the officers in Bin Laden's militia was Abdullah Azzam, a fundamentalist scholar who had been one of Bin Laden's teachers at a university in Saudi Arabia. Azzam embraced the ideas of Qutb, and it is likely he had a strong influence on Bin Laden.

The 2001 terrorist attacks on the World Trade Center and Pentagon did not end the threat in America. In 2007, five alleged mujahideen were arrested by federal authorities on charges of planning an attack on the Fort Dix military base in New Jersey. According to informants, the "Fort Dix Five" spent hours watching videos of Bin Laden encouraging would-be mujahideen to take up arms. One informant, Albanian immigrant Besnik Bakalli, recorded a conversation with defendants Dritan and Shain Duka in which they talked of seeing a video of a U.S. soldier shot while on patrol in Iraq. "They were happy," Bakalli said. "That's what we trained for—to kill soldiers."[24]

The Dukas, who are Albanian immigrants, as well as three other defendants, including their brother Eljvir, Jordanian Mohamad Shnewer, and Serdar Tatar, who was born in Turkey, were convicted in late 2008 on charges of conspiring to kill American soldiers.

Madrid Bombings

In some countries terrorism has helped fundamentalists achieve their goals. By taking lives and sending shock waves through the population, fundamentalists have been able to accomplish political change—although they may have to sacrifice their own lives or freedom for the cause.

> " Rumors . . . surfaced suggesting the Branch Davidians were stockpiling weapons. When federal agents showed up with a search warrant, a firefight broke out, resulting in the deaths of four agents and six cult members. "

In 2004 a terrorist strike by Islamic fundamentalists on commuter train stations in Madrid, Spain, killed 191 people. In the attack, members of a terrorist cell were convicted of filling backpacks with dynamite and nails, then exploding them aboard four commuter trains. Seven suspects killed themselves as police closed in on the apartment where they were hiding; 21 others were arrested and sentenced to lengthy prison terms.

Despite quick action by police to break the cell, the strike would seem to have fulfilled the terrorists' agenda. A year before the attack, Spain sent troops to Iraq to participate in the American-led invasion that ousted Saddam Hussein. In the months leading up to Spain's 2004 national election, an opposition party, the Spanish Socialist Workers, pledged to withdraw the troops if it prevailed.

The Socialist Workers were not expected to unseat the incumbent government, but three days before the election the terrorist cell exploded the bombs, horrifying the Spanish public. Spanish voters then sent a message to their government: They were clearly more interested in avoiding violence in their own country than in supporting the U.S. mission in Iraq. On election day, the Socialist Workers took power; their leader, José Luis Rodríguez Zapatero, took office as prime minister and weeks later ordered the Spanish troops home.

> " A Christian fundamentalist, Waagner declared that God had chosen him to wage war on abortion in the United States. "

The Branch Davidians

In some cases, a fundamentalist group's members do not seek to change the government or culture where they live, but they have established a society under their own rules that are in conflict with the laws of their host country. These fundamentalists often simply want to be left alone, and so when the authorities step in to enforce the law, the dispute can turn violent.

In 1993 Americans learned of the existence of an obscure fundamentalist splinter group of the Seventh-Day Adventist Church known as the Branch Davidians. Members lived on a ranch near Waco, Texas, where they awaited the apocalypse—the final confrontation between good and evil that would be followed by the appearance of Christ on Earth. In 1993 local officials heard rumors that the group's leader, David Koresh, had sexually assaulted minors at the ranch. Rumors also surfaced suggesting the Branch Davidians were stockpiling weapons. When federal agents showed up with a search warrant, a firefight broke out, resulting in the deaths of four agents and six cult members.

The incident led to a 51-day standoff that was finally broken when federal agents hurled tear gas canisters into the compound, sparking a fire that engulfed much of the cult's headquarters. When the fire died down, the agents found the bodies of 82 Davidians, including 29 children. Many of the cult members, including Koresh, died of single gunshot wounds to the head, suggesting they committed suicide rather than surrender to authorities.

Abortion Clinic Violence

Even when they are marginalized by society—thrown into jail or otherwise made to pay for their crimes—violent fundamentalists often maintain that their tactics are the only effective way to achieve their goals. In America abortion has been legal since the 1973 *Roe v. Wade* Supreme Court decision. Moreover, since then the federal government as well as the states have adopted laws protecting abortion clinic clients and staff members. And yet, violence at abortion clinics persists. According to the National Abortion Federation, nearly 10,000 acts of violence have been committed at abortion clinics in the 1990s and 2000s.

In 1994 Paul Hill, a defrocked minister, was convicted of murdering John Britton, a physician who performed abortions, as well as Britton's bodyguard. Hill was sentenced to death. Hill showed no remorse, telling interviewers that the only way to stop abortions in the United States is to kill abortionists. He was executed in 2003.

A more recent case involves Clayton Lee Waagner, who mailed nearly 300 envelopes purporting to contain anthrax spores to abortion clinics, Planned Parenthood offices, and other abortion rights activists. In reality, the envelopes contained harmless white powder, but people who opened the mail were terrorized. A Christian fundamentalist, Waagner declared that God had chosen him to wage war on abortion in the United States. "I'm a terrorist to a very narrow group of people, but a terrorist just the same," Waagner boasted. "As a terrorist to the abortionist, what I need to do is evoke terror. I wish to warn

> " During times of war in which the military drafted men into service, members of those churches often declared themselves 'conscientious objectors,' meaning they refused to take up arms because of their religious convictions. "

them that I am coming. I am anointed and called to be God's warrior."[25] Waagner was captured and, in 2005, sentenced to 19 years in prison.

Conscientious Objectors

The missions of Osama bin Laden, the Fort Dix Five, David Koresh, Paul Hill, and Clayton Lee Waagner would suggest that fundamentalists are willing to murder, terrorize, and die to spread their causes, but fundamentalist religion has another side. Leaders of many fundamentalist faiths also preach a pacifist message.

Among those faiths are the Amish, Mennonites, Seventh-Day Adventists, and the Jehovah's Witnesses. During times of war in which the military drafted men into service, members of those churches often declared themselves "conscientious objectors," meaning they refused to take up arms because of their religious or moral convictions. In many cases conscientious objectors still had to serve in the military but were given jobs as noncombatants, often as hospital workers. Sometimes religious fundamentalists defied the draft and would not even serve in noncombatant roles. In contrast to many of the fundamentalists of today who commit terrorism and incite violence, other fundamentalists have chosen to serve in prison rather than aim weapons at other human beings.

Primary Source Quotes*

Does Religious Fundamentalism Fuel Violence and Terrorism?

66 Islam condemns all forms of terrorist attacks. According to the Qur'an, it is a great sin to kill an innocent person, and anyone who does so will suffer great torment in the Hereafter. 99

—Hassan Isilow, "Islam Denounces Terrorism," *Kampala Monitor* (Uganda), April 22, 2007.

Isilow is a Muslim and journalist based in South Africa.

66 Allah Most High has obligated believers to battle all those who reject Him, the Exalted, until all chaos ceases and all religion belongs to Allah. . . . Among those needing to be fought at this day and age are those rulers who govern people without the sharia—they who fight against the people of Islam, who befriend the infidels from among the Jews, Christians, and others. 99

—Ayman al-Zawahiri, "Jihad, Martyrdom, and the Killing of Innocents," in *The Al-Qaeda Reader,* ed. and trans. Raymond Ibrahim. New York: Doubleday, 2007.

Born in Egypt, Al-Zawahiri is a physician and chief lieutenant to al Qaeda leader Osama bin Laden.

Bracketed quotes indicate conflicting positions.

* Editor's Note: While the definition of a primary source can be narrowly or broadly defined, for the purposes of Compact Research, a primary source consists of: 1) results of original research presented by an organization or researcher; 2) eyewitness accounts of events, personal experience, or work experience; 3) first-person editorials offering pundits' opinions; 4) government officials presenting political plans and/or policies; 5) representatives of organizations presenting testimony or policy.

Primary Source Quotes

❝It may be assumed that the great majority of Muslims in the world have no desire to embark on a jihad of any sort against the West. Moderate Muslims argue that jihad in Islam should be interpreted as a spiritual rather than a military struggle and that the paradigm of the prophet Muhammad should inspire his followers to tolerance, leniency, love for humankind, and the rejection of terrorism.❞

—Shmuel Bar, *Warrant for Terror: The Fatwas of Radical Islam and the Duty of Jihad.* Lanham, MD: Rowman & Littlefield, 2006.

Bar is director of studies, Institute of Policy and Strategy, Herzliya, Israel.

❝In concrete terms jihadis believe that their mission is to implement their version of Islam, including the imperative to carry out warfare against the unbelievers, and all the troubles of the Islamic world will disappear.❞

—Mary Habeck, *Knowing the Enemy: Jihadist Ideology and the War on Terror.* New Haven, CT: Yale University Press, 2006.

Habeck is associate professor, School of Advanced International Studies, Johns Hopkins University.

❝The bombers are happy because they are abandoning this world of disgrace and shame for one where they are venerated along with the honorable and righteous believers, enjoying for eternity all the fruits of their sacrifice. As proof of such happiness, jihadists often post on the Web photos of dead jihadists who appear to be smiling or peacefully asleep.❞

—Mohammad M. Hafez, *Suicide Bombers in Iraq: The Strategy and Ideology of Martyrdom.* Washington, DC: United States Institute of Peace, 2007.

Hafez is a professor of political science at the University of Missouri–Kansas City.

"Like other forms of religious fundamentalism, Christian fundamentalism is a dreaded doctrine of supremacy, a cult of hatred, and a recipe for disaster."

—Yoginder Sikand, "Christian Fundamentalism and American Empire,"
Countercurrents.org, September 24, 2006. www.countercurrents.org.

Sikand works with the Centre for Jawaharlal Nehru Studies, Jamia Millia Islamia, New Delhi, India.

....

"Fundamentalists are militant in fighting against any challenge to their beliefs. They are often angry and sometimes resort to verbal or even physical abuse against those who interfere with the implementation of their agenda."

—Jimmy Carter, *Our Endangered Values: America's Moral Crisis.* New York: Simon & Schuster, 2005.

Carter is the thirty-ninth president of the United States.

....

"Unfortunately, as with all anti-abortion cases where the defenders of the innocents are charged with crimes and brought before the judges in this land, there is no consideration given to the 'defense of necessity'—that these interventions were necessary because a true human being is murdered in every intentional abortion."

—Michael Bray, "Pardon Me Boys, but You Need to 'Pardon' Rachelle Shannon," October 23, 2008. www.michaelbray.org.

Bray, of Wilmington, Ohio, is a Lutheran minister who has been jailed in abortion clinic violence cases.

....

> 66 To the anti-abortion movement, standing outside clinic doors and bellowing at patients and staff that they are murderers and whores is simply an effort to 'stop the war against America's children.' Like most wars, this one has included a host of tactics, from picket lines to blockades, and has gone so far as to include arson, property damage, kidnapping and the murder of providers. 99

—Eleanor J. Bader, "Anti-Abortion Tactics Take a Toll," *On the Issues,* Fall 2008. www.ontheissuesmagazine.com.

Bader is author of the book *Targets of Hatred: Anti-Abortion Terrorism.*

Facts and Illustrations

Does Religious Fundamentalism Fuel Violence and Terrorism?

- According to the National Abortion Federation, abortion providers in the United States and Canada received **39 death threats, 49 bomb threats**, and **2,412 pieces of hate mail or harassing phone calls** between 2004 and 2008.

- In 2007 nearly **100 mosques** were targeted for violence by Islamic extremists, according to the National Counterterrorism Center.

- The U.S. State Department has identified **44 groups** it considers **foreign terrorist organizations**; of those, 31 are affiliated with fundamentalist religious movements.

- The India Ministry of State has reported that more than **50 terrorist training camps** are in Pakistan and as many as **172** operating in Bangladesh; the two countries are home to large populations of Islamic fundamentalists.

- More than **150 terrorist attacks** occurred in Pakistan in 2007, a **137 percent** increase over 2006; most occurred in the Pakistan-Afghanistan border region where the Islamic fundamentalist Taliban has regrouped since its ouster from the Afghan government in 2001.

- Despite its decision to withdraw troops from Iraq, Spain is still confronted by Islamic terrorists; in 2007 Spanish authorities arrested **47 suspected terrorists** with ties to fundamentalist Islamic cells.

Many Muslims Oppose Suicide Bombings

Many Muslims are coming to believe that suicide bombing in defense of Islam is wrong. According to a 2008 poll, the number of Muslims in Lebanon who believe suicide bombing is justified dropped from 74 percent in 2002 to 32 percent in 2008. Suicide bombing is also falling out of favor among Muslims in Pakistan, Jordan, and other countries as well.

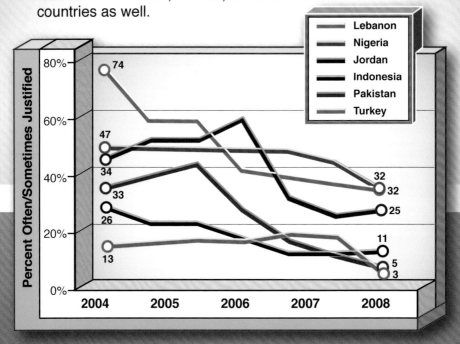

Source: Pew Global Attitudes Project, "Global Public Opinion in the Bush Years," December 18, 2008. http://pewglobal.org.

- Osama bin Laden has issued a "State of Jihad" declaration in which he included 20 objectives and assertions, the last of which called for **Muslims to give their lives for jihad.**

- The Gallup Organization asked 10,000 Muslims in four Islamic countries—Lebanon, Kuwait, Jordan, and Morocco—to define **"jihad;"** Gallup received so many different answers that the pollster concluded the word **could not be defined in any clear way.**

- Six months before Islamic fundamentalists staged attacks in Mumbai, India, that killed **171 people** in late 2008, a poll in India found **22 percent** of people believed Islamic violence against Hindus would continue to escalate.

- Al Qaeda in Mesopotamia, an Islamic fundamentalist group in Iraq, committed more than **40 acts of terror** in 2007, killing more than **170 people**. More than 120 of the deaths resulted from **suicide bombings**.

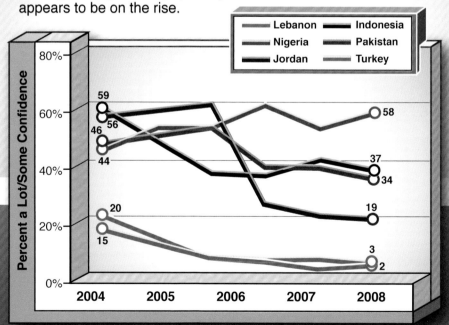

Muslim Confidence in Osama bin Laden Waning in the Islamic World

Seven years after the September 11, 2001, attacks on Washington and New York, support for the attacks' mastermind, Osama bin Laden, has waned in many Islamic countries. Support for Bin Laden in Jordan reached a peak of more than 60 percent in 2005, but by 2008 just 19 percent of Jordanian Muslims supported the al Qaeda leader. Support for Bin Laden has fallen in other Islamic countries, although in Nigeria his popularity appears to be on the rise.

Source: Pew Global Attitudes Project, "Global Public Opinion in the Bush Years," December 18, 2008. http://pewglobal.org.

Abortion Clinics Under Attack

Although abortion clinic workers have occasionally been murdered, assaulted, and kidnapped, trespassing and vandalism are the most frequent crimes committed against the clinics. Many of the illegal actions against the clinics are committed by fundamentalist Christians who oppose abortions. Statistics also show that abortion opponents harass clinic workers, often over the phone or through the Internet.

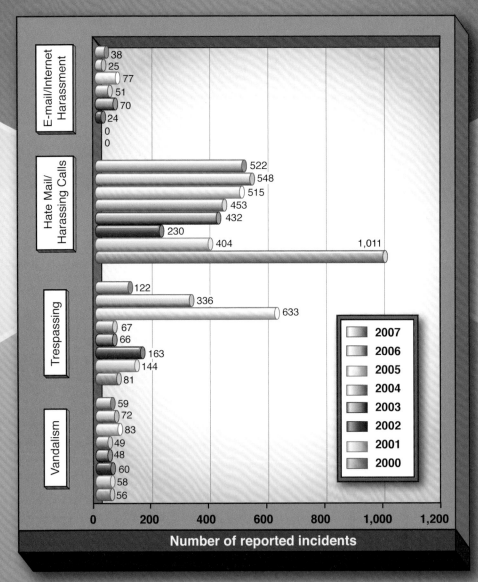

Source: National Abortion Federation, "NAF Violence and Disruption Statistics," 2008. www.prochoice.org.

How Should Governments Respond to Religious Fundamentalism?

Governments often respond to fundamentalist movements with heavy-handed tactics. Across the globe, regimes have watched nervously as fundamentalists gain popular support and declare their intentions to seize power. Frequently, regimes respond by ordering crackdowns aimed at silencing the fundamentalists, often through the use of imprisonment, banishment, and torture.

In Egypt, President Hosni Mubarak has long regarded the fundamentalist Muslim Brotherhood as a threat. Mubarak has occasionally ordered members of the brotherhood tossed into prisons, but the movement's leaders refuse to go away. Some Middle East analysts fear that fundamentalists in Egypt will eventually seize power and install an Islamic republic similar to the theocracy in Iran. Says Egyptian American human rights activist Saad Eddin Ibrahim, "Though it has been banned for many years, the Brotherhood has been a pervasive presence throughout Egypt, enduring despite attacks from the state-controlled media, periodic arrests and protracted detentions of its members."[26]

Since coming to power in 1981 Mubarak has deployed the army and police agencies to silence his critics. Many believe that Mubarak, now in his eighties, will soon step aside so that his son Gamal can ascend to the presidency. A former investments banker in Great Britain, Gamal Mubarak favors maintaining relations with the West. In Egypt, fundamentalist leaders are already seething over the prospect of Gamal Mubarak taking power. "I categorically reject Gamal Mubarak,"[27] declares Muslim Brotherhood leader Mahdi Akif. Egypt is likely to remain a volatile country for many years as its leaders wrestle with the rise of fundamentalism.

> " In Egypt, President Hosni Mubarak has long regarded the fundamentalist Muslim Brotherhood as a threat. Mubarak has occasionally ordered members of the Brotherhood tossed into prisons, but the movement's leaders refuse to go away. "

Meanwhile, other governments also struggle to remain stable against incursions by fundamentalists. Indonesia has made it clear to Islamic fundamentalists that violence will not be tolerated—it has tried and executed mujahideen responsible for taking lives. Following the 2008 attacks by an Islamic group in Mumbai, India, the governments of Pakistan and India set aside their long-standing differences to hunt down the killers.

Executions in Indonesia

Some governments deal harshly with terrorism sparked by fundamentalist causes. In 2008 Indonesia executed Islamic fundamentalists who were convicted in the bombing of a nightclub in Bali that killed 202 people. Put to death were brothers Amrozi and Mukhlas bin Hasyim and an accomplice, Imam Samudra. The extremists were members of the terrorist cell Jemaah Islamiah, which maintained links with al Qaeda.

After their convictions, the mujahideen said they picked the nightclub because they knew it was frequented by non-Muslims—the death toll included 88 Australians and 38 Britons, targeted because their homelands are part of the coalition of North Atlantic Treaty Organization forces seeking to eliminate Taliban guerillas in Afghanistan. "My only mission was to help the Muslims,"[28] insisted Samudra.

Meanwhile, fundamentalism appears to be growing more powerful in the country. Indonesia has an Islamic majority—86 percent of the country's 237 million people are Muslims. Fundamentalists have used the democratic process to gain influence—the Justice Welfare Party (JWP), which was modeled after the Muslim Brotherhood, controls a handful of seats in the Indonesian parliament. The JWP is still in a minority in the legislature, but across Indonesia many women wear *hijabs* while several mosques have adopted Wahhabism. Secularists fear that in future elections the fundamentalists will find more widespread support. Even as the Bali bombers faced the firing squad, rallies were held throughout the country supporting them. Said Yenny Zannuba Wahid, an adviser to Indonesian president Susilo Bambang Yudhoyono, "The religious agenda is shaping more and more areas of daily life."[29]

Displaying the Ten Commandments

When fundamentalists attempt to exert their influence over a society, democratic governments have relied on the courts to assess whether their ideas or programs are permitted under law. Such tests are often decided on a case by case basis because a fine line exists between the freedom to worship and the principles held by governments outlawing state support for religion.

Fundamentalist Christians in America have often supported displaying monuments to the Ten Commandments on public property, prompting the courts to decide whether these displays violate the separation of church and state doctrine of the Constitution. In 2005 the U.S. Supreme Court ruled that a plaque displaying the Ten Commandments on the grounds of the Texas capitol in Austin did not represent state promotion of a religion. The Court

> " When fundamentalists attempt to exert their influence over a society, democratic governments have relied on the courts to assess whether their ideas or programs are permitted under law. "

found that the monument had been donated to the capitol not by a church or other group with a religious agenda, but by an Elks lodge. The Court ruled the display of the Ten Commandments was not erected to convey a religious message and, therefore, the monument was permitted to remain on the capitol grounds.

In another case, though, the Court did rule that display of the Ten Commandments on public property was prompted by religious fervor. Soon after taking office in 2001, the chief judge of the Alabama Supreme Court, Roy Moore, ordered a granite monument to the Ten Commandments placed in front of the court's building in the state capital of Montgomery. In response, a federal judge found that the monument violated the First Amendment and ordered it removed.

Moore had a long history of fundamental Christian activism—he had already displayed the Ten Commandments in his courtroom and often led jurors in Christian prayers before convening court. Moore responded to the federal court order by defying it—he refused to have the monument removed. "It is a sad day in our country when the moral foundation of our law and the acknowledgment of God have to be hidden from public view to appease a federal judge,"[30] Moore insisted. After refusing to abide by the court order, Moore was kicked out of office by an Alabama judicial panel. Meanwhile, his granite monument to the Ten Commandments was hauled away.

> " The [Justice Welfare Party] is still in a minority in the legislature, but across Indonesia many women wear *hijabs* while several mosques have adopted Wahhabism. "

Reforming Laws

In addition to the courts, other branches of government can be employed to respond to the influence of fundamentalists. Laws are constantly written, refined, and strengthened by legislators to help clarify and define separation of church and state issues.

In 2009 Congress responded to America's recession by adopting a stimulus program designed to pump $787 billion into the economy. Included in the package was a provision to spend billions of dollars on school reconstruction projects. When the legislation was written, it specified that the money could not be used to fund reconstruction of schools owned by churches or by schools that permit prayer meetings on campus. U.S. senator Jim DeMint of South Carolina attempted to strike that provision from the legislation, thereby permitting the stimulus money to be used to rebuild religious schools. DeMint, a fundamentalist Christian, said, "This provision is a clear attack on people of faith and it must be removed."[31] When the Senate voted on the provision it was upheld by a 54-43 margin, thereby ensuring that the stimulus money would not be used to fund schools that teach fundamentalism or any other form of religious expression.

America is not the only country where laws and policies are constantly reviewed and altered in response to fundamentalist influences. In Saudi Arabia, King Abdullah authorized reforms when he believed fundamentalists had infringed on individual rights. In 2009 Abdullah fired the head of the country's religious court, the Supreme Judicial Council, after Saleh al Lihedan proclaimed that it was permissible to kill TV executives who authorize broadcasts of "immoral" content. A moderate cleric was appointed in his place.

Also replaced was the head of the religious police force, the Commission to Promote Virtue and Prevent Vice. The new head has declared that he is more interested in forgiveness than in punishment and that those accused of violating sharia law would be considered innocent until proven guilty. It is a concept with a long history in America, but in Saudi Arabia, where alleged violators have been administered punishment on the spot, the presumption of innocence represents a break with strict fundamentalism. "This is the true start

> " The chief judge of the Alabama Supreme Court, Roy Moore, ordered a granite monument to the Ten Commandments placed in front of the court's building in the state capital of Montgomery. In response, a federal judge found that the monument violated the First Amendment and ordered it removed. "

of the promises of reform," said Jamal Khashoggi, a Saudi journalist. "[The moderates] bring not only new blood, but also new ideas."[32]

Rights in the Balance

Sometimes governments find they must balance the rights of fundamentalists to practice their faiths against the rights of others to be protected under law. This can often become a complicated matter because fundamentalists adhere to customs and ideals that are often centuries old, predating modern laws written by secular lawmakers.

In 2008 child welfare authorities in Texas raided a compound maintained by the Fundamentalist Church of Jesus Christ of Latter Day Saints, a splinter group of the Mormon church, after receiving reports that girls as young as 13 were forced into marriages with adult men. Moreover, the church accepted the practice of polygamy, which is illegal in all 50 states. Twelve adults were charged with sexual assault and related offenses involving minor girls.

Initially, more than 400 children were taken into protective custody because authorities feared for their safety. At home, Americans followed the case in the press, which published and broadcast images of the female members of the church dressed in ankle-length, nineteenth-century-style clothes.

Eventually, a handful of church members were charged with crimes, while most of the children were returned to their parents after authorities determined they were not in danger. The case illustrates that the government felt obligated to intervene in a fundamentalist community that had set itself apart, electing to adhere to its own rules and customs. Ultimately, most of the fundamentalists were permitted to return to the way of life they preferred because the government was obligated to observe their rights as well.

> "Child welfare authorities in Texas raided a compound maintained by the Fundamentalist Church of Jesus Christ of Latter Day Saints, a splinter group of the Mormon church, after receiving reports that girls as young as 13 were forced into marriages with adult men."

Use of Force

The most volatile corners of the planet feature clashes between fundamentalists and those who are governed by secular principles. In those cases, fundamentalists represent a threat to peace. Governments find themselves employing diplomatic efforts, forging alliances and authorizing the use of force to respond to fundamentalist threats.

During the administration of President George W. Bush the United States contemplated launching a military strike against Iran because the Islamic republic has pursued a program to develop nuclear weapons. To many American leaders, the notion of permitting an unstable fundamentalist Islamic regime access to nuclear weapons is unthinkable. By 2009 the administration of President Barack Obama hoped to use negotiations, rather than the threat of an attack, to convince the Iranians to drop their nuclear arms program. Clearly, though, American diplomats are well aware of the stakes, knowing the devastation that Iran could cause if its mullahs choose to use nuclear arms to wage jihad.

The neighboring states of India and Pakistan have long harbored suspicions of one another—each nation includes radical elements that have launched terrorist attacks. However, following the terrorist attack in the Indian city of Mumbai that took 171 lives in late 2008, the two governments cooperated in the investigation. Soon, Pakistani authorities announced the arrests of leaders of a fundamentalist Islamic group known as Lashkar-e-Tayyiba (in English, the Army of the Righteous). The Pakistan-based group aims to establish India as an Islamic republic, meaning that it seeks the annihilation of millions of Hindus.

To help the two governments cooperate, agents from the U.S. Central Intelligence Agency (CIA) acted as intermediaries. Meanwhile, Pakistan has become a close ally of the United States, which maintains troops in neighboring Afghanistan in the ongoing war against the Taliban. The

> " The Islamic fundamentalists have been carrying out a long-term guerilla war against American troops and have crossed the border into Pakistan where they have influenced life in rural villages. "

Islamic fundamentalists have been carrying out a long-term guerilla war against American troops and have crossed the border into Pakistan where they have influenced life in rural villages. In the border region the Taliban has imposed its strict version of Islam—beheading violators of sharia, forcing women to wear burkas, and blowing up schools that permit girls to enroll. At this point American diplomats harbor fears that Islamic fundamentalists will eventually gain the upper hand in Pakistan and take over the government.

As American troops in Afghanistan, Iraq, and other volatile corners of the planet have learned, Islamic fundamentalists have proven many times they are willing to die and kill others to spread jihad. Other fundamentalists have also turned to violence from time to time. In America, though, the Constitution defends individual rights—even the rights of people who believe religious principles should take precedence over secular laws. As fundamentalists pursue their goals, national leaders know they must be vigilant when protecting Americans, but they also realize they must seek a greater understanding of why fundamentalists often turn to such drastic measures to protect their way of life.

Primary Source Quotes*

How Should Governments Respond to Religious Fundamentalism?

> 66 The simplest way to stabilize [Afghanistan] may be to negotiate a truce with the Taliban fundamentalists who were driven from power by the United States in 2001. The question policymakers are pondering, in fact, isn't whether to negotiate with the Taliban but when. 99

—David Ignatius, "Tea with the Taliban?" *Washington Post*, October 26, 2008.

Ignatius is a columnist for the *Washington Post*.

> 66 Since 2001, the Taliban's brutal insurgency has sought to destroy Afghanistan's emerging democracy. It ruthlessly murders Afghan men, women and children, blows up schools, and destroys the infrastructure critical for modernizing Afghanistan. With the Taliban's record, what concessions could the government reasonably concede? Any negotiations involving Washington would undermine U.S. credibility. 99

—William C. Martel, "Fanatics Don't Compromise," *USA Today*, October 29, 2008.

Martel is associate professor of international security studies at the Fletcher School at Tufts University in Massachusetts.

Bracketed quotes indicate conflicting positions.

* Editor's Note: While the definition of a primary source can be narrowly or broadly defined, for the purposes of Compact Research, a primary source consists of: 1) results of original research presented by an organization or researcher; 2) eyewitness accounts of events, personal experience, or work experience; 3) first-person editorials offering pundits' opinions; 4) government officials presenting political plans and/or policies; 5) representatives of organizations presenting testimony or policy.

Primary Source Quotes

"A war on terror is inherently unwinnable as a military exercise. . . . Unmasking the underlying ideological framework of an extreme religious fundamentalism is the first step in formulating a countering ideology."

—Douglas Pratt, "Terrorism and Religious Fundamentalism: Prospects for a Predictive Paradigm," *Marburg Journal of Religion,* June 2006.

Pratt is associate professor of philosophy and religious studies, University of Waikato, New Zealand.

"The United States and other countries must . . . find reasonable strategies that will exploit the failures of the jihadis, stop the extremists from carrying out violent attacks, minimize the appeal of their beliefs, and eventually end their war with the world."

—Mary Habeck, *Knowing the Enemy: Jihadist Ideology and the War on Terror.* New Haven, CT: Yale University Press, 2006.

Habeck is associate professor, School of Advanced International Studies, Johns Hopkins University.

"The challenge for America and the West is that we must try to, more or less, simultaneously shield our nations from the Islamists; strengthen our own cultural vigor, laws, and military capacity; and shrewdly intervene in the Islamic world to establish healthy economic and political connections."

—Tony Blankley, *The West's Last Chance: Will We Win the Clash of Civilizations?* Washington DC: Regnery, 2005.

Blankley is the editorial page editor of the *Washington Times* and a regular panelist on *The McLaughlin Group.*

66 Terrorist organizations . . . have become especially expert at manipulating the Internet to their advantage. . . . Western governments and others involved in counterterrorism efforts will need to become at least as innovative, aggressive, and progressive in their approach to the Internet in order to counter the enemy who fully intends to employ this medium against us.99

—Steve Emerson and the Investigative Project on Terrorism, *Jihad Incorporated: A Guide to Militant Islam in the U.S.* Amherst, NY: Prometheus, 2006.

Emerson is an internationally recognized expert on terrorism and national security and founder and executive director of the Investigative Project on Terrorism, which maintains the largest nongovernmental data and intelligence library in the world on militant Islam.

66 We are engaged in a basic struggle, a struggle between humanity and inhumanity, between builders and destroyers. If fighting these people and preventing the export of their brand of radicalism and terror is not intrinsic to the national security and most cherished values of the United States, I don't know what is.99

—John McCain, remarks on Iraq delivered at the Virginia Military Institute, CQ Transcripts Wire, April 11, 2007. www.washingtonpost.com.

McCain is a U.S. senator from Arizona and was the Republican candidate for president in 2008.

66 Unless the Bangladesh government acts to crack down on extremism and terrorism, the potential threat that Islamic extremism in Bangladesh poses to global security could turn imminent.99

—Sudha Ramachandran, "The Threat of Islamic Extremism to Bangladesh," *PINR (Power Interest News Report)*, July 27, 2005. www.pinr.com.

Ramachandran is a writer in Bangalore, India, who specializes in terrorism and conflict zones. She has a doctoral degree from the School of International Studies, Jawaharlal Nehru University, in New Delhi.

❝The divisiveness of religion in current public life is inescapable. This is no time to deny the prudence of understanding the [First Amendment] to require the government to stay neutral on religious belief, which is reserved for the conscience of the individual.❞

—David H. Souter, majority opinion, *McCreary County, Kentucky et al., v. American Civil Liberties Union of Kentucky et al.,* U.S. Supreme Court, June 6, 2005. http://supreme.justia.com.

Souter is a justice of the U.S. Supreme Court.

❝Those who wrote the Constitution believed that morality was essential to the well-being of society and that encouragement of religion was the best way to foster morality. The fact that the founding fathers believed devotedly that there was a God and that the unalienable rights of man were rooted in him is clearly evidenced in their writings, from the Mayflower Compact to the Constitution itself.❞

—Justice Antonin Scalia, dissenting opinion, *McCreary County, Kentucky et al., v. American Civil Liberties Union of Kentucky et al.,* U.S. Supreme Court, June 6, 2005. http://supreme.justia.com.

Scalia is a justice of the U.S. Supreme Court.

❝If religious beliefs about the dignity of human life were illegitimate as a basis for public policy, there would have been no abolition or civil rights movements. The idea of a divine image found in every human person is one of the main foundations for the American tradition of liberty, tolerance and pluralism.❞

—Michael Gerson, "Faith-Based Condescension," *Washington Post,* Sept. 12, 2008.

Gerson is a columnist for the *Washington Post.*

❝The United States Constitution in its First Amendment disestablishes religion and creates what would become known, in Thomas Jefferson's famous phrase, as a 'wall of separation' between church and state. Whatever their political ambitions, American fundamentalists are constrained by this wall.❞

—Malise Ruthven, *Fundamentalism: A Very Short Introduction.* Oxford, England: Oxford University Press, 2007.

Ruthven is an author and former history professor at the University of Aberdeen in Scotland who specializes in religious studies.

How Should Governments Respond to Religious Fundamentalism?

- When candidates from the fundamentalist **Muslim Brotherhood** were poised to make significant gains in the Egyptian parliament in the 2005 elections, President Hosni Mubarak had nearly 500 of the group's leaders thrown into prisons.

- King Abdullah of Saudi Arabia took steps in 2009 to **reduce the influence of Islamic fundamentalists in Arabian life** by ousting several hardline clerics from the Grand Ulama Commission, which is composed of Islamic scholars whose duties include interpreting the sharia. Abdullah filled their slots with moderate scholars.

- According to a poll taken after a federal judge ordered the removal of the Ten Commandments monument from in front of the Alabama Supreme Court building, **77 percent** of Americans believed the monument should have remained in place.

- Just **18 percent** of Americans favor a military strike against Iran to halt that country's nuclear arms development program; in contrast, **73 percent** of Americans believe the U.S. government should pursue a diplomatic resolution with the fundamentalist Islamic nation.

- Pakistan deployed **120,000 troops** to its border region with Afghanistan in February 2009 to root out the fundamentalist Taliban guerillas that infiltrated the countryside.

Support for Military Action Against Iran Declining

People in many countries would rather see their diplomats negotiate with Iran's fundamentalist Islamic regime than initiate tough measures to convince the Iranians to drop their nuclear arms development program. Such measures could include severe economic sanctions—such as refusing to buy Iranian oil—or even military action. Moreover, pollsters found support for economic sanctions or military action has waned since the questions were last asked in 2006. Some 21,000 people in 21 countries responded to the 2008 poll.

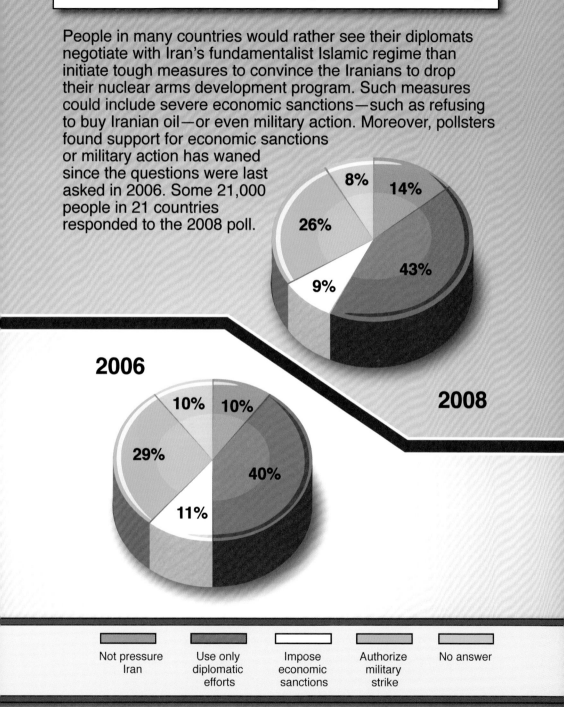

2006

2008

Not pressure Iran

Use only diplomatic efforts

Impose economic sanctions

Authorize military strike

No answer

Source: WorldPublicOpinion.org, "Declining Support for Tough Measures Against Iran's Nuclear Program: Global Poll," March 11, 2008. www.worldpublicopinion.org.

Should Churches Attempt to Influence Public Policy?

Majorities of the memberships of evangelical Christian churches as well as black churches, both of whom tend to embrace fundamentalism, believe their churches should take active roles in public policy and try to influence governments by speaking out on such issues as abortion and same-sex marriage, according to a study by the Pew Forum on Religion and Public Life. In all other faiths, members who feel their churches should address public policy issues are in the minority.

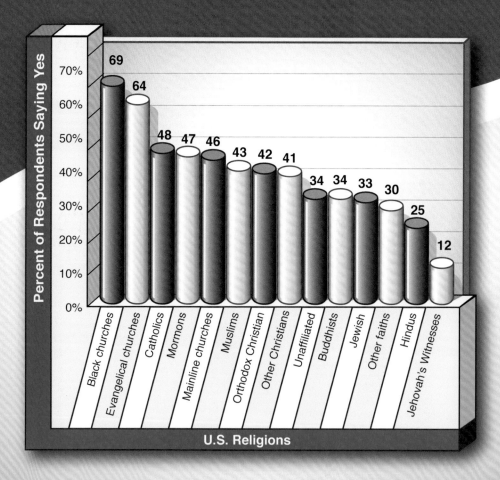

Source: Pew Forum on Religion and Public Life, "U.S. Religious Landscape Survey, February 2008. http://religions.pewforum.org.

Should Religious Symbols Be Displayed on Public Property?

While evangelicals are strong supporters of religious displays and prayer in public settings, a 2008 poll found that a majority of the general U.S. population shares these views. The poll, conducted by Ellison Research, found that Americans believe displays of nativity scenes and other religious symbols on public property should be legal. The poll also found that Americans believe prayers should be legal in public school classrooms and school wide events.

Perceptions of what should be legal
(regardless of whether it is currently legal)

Situation	Should be legal	Should be illegal
The display of a Nativity scene on city property, such as a city hall, during Christmas	83%	17%
The display of a scene honoring Islam on city property, such as a city hall, during Ramadan (a Muslim holiday)	60%	40%
The display of the Ten Commandments inside a court building	79%	21%
Voluntary student-led prayers at public school events, such as football games or graduation ceremonies	87%	13%
A public school teacher permitting a "moment of silence" for prayer or contemplation for all students during class time	89%	11%
Religious groups renting public property, such as a public school gym or a library room, for meetings if nonreligious groups are allowed to do so	90%	10%
A public school teacher wearing a religious symbol such as a cross or a Star of David during class time	88%	12%

Source: Ellison Research, "Liberals and Conservatives Both Want Freedom of Religious Expression and Practice," January 10, 2008. http://ellisonresearch.com.

- Due to setbacks in the war against the Taliban in Afghanistan, in early 2009 the United States announced it would send an additional **17,000 troops** to the country, bringing the total U.S. troops in Afghanistan to **55,000**.

- Despite opposition to his 2008 election by fundamentalist Christians, President Barack Obama invited a fundamentalist minister, Rick Warren of Saddleback Church in California, to deliver the invocation at his inauguration in early 2009. By inviting Warren, Obama said he hoped to **open a dialogue with fundamentalists**.

- The Texas Supreme Court ruled in May 2008 that the state's Department of Family and Protective Services had violated the rights of members of the Fundamentalist Church of Jesus Christ of Latter-Day Saints by **removing 468 children** from their parents' custody. The court ordered the children returned to their families.

- Although American courts have consistently barred prayer in public schools, a 2001 U.S. Supreme Court ruling found that a fundamentalist group known as the Good News Club could hold **after-school Bible study** classes in public school buildings.

- To maintain the secular integrity of its public schools, in 2004 **France banned overtly religious attire worn by fundamentalists** and others, including hijabs worn by Muslim girls, turbans worn by Sikhs, large crosses worn by Christians, and skullcaps worn by Jews.

Key People and Advocacy Groups

Osama bin Laden: Founder and financier of the terrorist network al Qaeda, the fugitive Saudi Arabian millionaire is wanted for spearheading the terrorist attacks of September 11, 2001, that killed more than 3,000 people in New York, Washington, D.C., and rural Pennsylvania. Bin Laden turned to fundamentalist Islam while serving as one of the mujahideen during the Soviet Union's occupation of Afghanistan.

Richard Dawkins: The British biologist has led the New Atheist movement, campaigning against the influence of religion in public life, particularly scientific research. Dawkins, author of *The God Delusion*, focuses much of his criticism on Christian fundamentalists who have tried to insert creationist theories into the science of evolution.

Ruqaya al Ghasara: At the 2008 Summer Olympics, the sprinter from Bahrain insisted on wearing the *hijab* and a full body suit to comply with her country's conservative interpretation of Islamic law. Running alongside athletes clad in shorts and tank tops, Al Ghasara has become an international symbol of the modern Islamic woman who can still compete on an even plane with others while also observing sharia law.

Ayaan Hirsi Ali: Born in Somalia, the Muslim woman partnered with Theo van Gogh to produce the film *Submission,* which alleged ill treatment of women under Islamic law. After the film was broadcast on Dutch TV, Islamic fundamentalists railed against the film, which led to Van Gogh's murder. Hirsi Ali has remained active in the Islamic reform movement and has served in the Dutch parliament.

Meir Kahane: The founder of the Jewish Defense League, Kahane promoted the use of violence against enemies of Judaism. After serving a prison term in a bomb-making case, Kahane settled in Israel where he founded a political party that espoused racist ideology. He was assassinated in 1990 by an Islamic militant from Egypt.

Ayatollah Ruhollah Khomeini: The fundamentalist Muslim cleric's followers led a coup that took over the government of Iran in 1979. Khomeini had been in exile but returned to establish an Islamic republic based on a strict interpretation of sharia. By the time he died in 1989, Khomeini had established a regime hostile to America and most other Western states.

Lily Mazahery: The Iranian American attorney is founder of the Legal Rights Institute in Washington, D.C., which campaigns for an end to punishment by stoning and other human rights abuses in Iran.

Roy Moore: As the chief justice of the Alabama Supreme Court, Moore ordered a monument to the Ten Commandments erected in front of the supreme court's building in Montgomery, Alabama. When Moore defied a federal court order to have the monument removed, an Alabama judicial review panel removed him from the bench.

Operation Save America: Operation Save America is one of the chief antiabortion rights groups in the United States. The organization often invokes fundamentalist Christian doctrine during its crusades to close abortion clinics.

People for the American Way: The national organization tracks fundamentalist religious influences in American schools, government, and culture and helps campaign for principles opposed by fundamentalists, including legalization of same-sex marriage.

Rashtriya Swayamsevak Sangh: The fundamentalist Hindu sect in India has advocated violence against Muslims. RSS is believed to have some 4.5 million followers and has won election to a majority of seats in the state legislature of Gujarat, India.

Robert and Mary Schindler: The parents of Terri Schiavo waged a seven-year court battle to prevent the brain-dead woman's husband from removing her feeding tube. When the Schindlers' legal options were exhausted, Christian fundamentalist leaders lobbied Congress and President George W. Bush to give federal courts authority to review the case. Although the emergency legislation passed, federal judges still found that Michael Schiavo had the right to have the feeding tube removed from his wife.

Malkie Schwartz: Raised in a Hasidic Jewish home, Schwartz rebelled against the principles of fundamentalist Judaism, which required her to marry and devote herself entirely to her husband and children. After leaving home, Schwartz earned a college degree and established Footsteps, an organization that helps Jews who have left Hasidism adjust to contemporary life.

Nouriya al-Subeeh: The education minister of Kuwait has refused to wear the *hajib* or a veil in public, raising objections from the country's Islamic clerics. Al-Subeeh maintains that it is the right of Islamic women to decide for themselves how they wish to dress.

Chronology

1979
The Soviet Union invades Afghanistan, prompting thousands of Muslims to volunteer as mujahideen—soldiers who fight in the defense of Islam.

600s
Muhammad recites the words of the god Allah, becoming the prophet of Islam. He remains the most revered figure in the history of Islam.

1968
Meir Kahane, a New York rabbi, founds the Jewish Defense League. Kahane advocates the use of violence in retaliation for oppressive or violent acts against Jews. Kahane is assassinated by an Islamic fundamentalist in 1990.

1989
As the Soviets withdraw from Afghanistan, Osama bin Laden, a leader of the mujahideen, establishes al Qaeda to defend other Islamic lands against invasion by infidels.

1950
Pope Piux XII issues an encyclical finding no conflict between Catholic beliefs and Darwinism.

1928
The fundamentalist Muslim Brotherhood is established in Egypt.

1910	1930	1950	1970	1990

1964
Ayatollah Ruhollah Khomeini is exiled from Iran; the fundamentalist Islamic cleric will return to his country in 1979 to establish an Islamic republic.

1981
Egyptian president Anwar Sadat is assassinated by Islamic fundamentalists who oppose his peace overtures to Israel.

1967
Israel seizes the West Bank from Jordan during the Six Day War. Later, communities of fundamentalist Jews will establish settlements in the West Bank and refuse to leave as Israel makes plans to turn the territory over to the Palestinians.

1973
The U.S. Supreme Court hands down the *Roe v. Wade* decision, making abortion legal in America. Despite the Court's decision, fundamentalist Christians mount a campaign to oppose abortion by blocking clinic entrances and often resorting to violent tactics.

1700s
Islamic scholar Muhammad ibn-Abdul Wahhab preaches a conservative form of Islam that will become known as Wahhabism. Eventually, Wahhabism becomes the dominant form of Islam practiced in Saudi Arabia.

1993
Eighty-two members of the Branch Davidians, a fundamentalist Christian cult, die in a confrontation with federal agents at the cult's compound near Waco, Texas.

1994
Congress passes a law making it illegal to block the access of clients to abortion clinics.

1998
Michael Schiavo, husband of Terri Schiavo, receives court permission to have the feeding tube removed from the brain-dead woman, setting off a seven-year court battle in which fundamentalist Christians fight to keep Terri Schiavo alive.

2001
More than 3,000 Americans die when airplanes hijacked by Islamic fundamentalists recruited by al Qaeda slam into the World Trade Center in New York, the Pentagon in Washington, D.C., and a rural field in Pennsylvania.

2004
Voters in Spain oust an incumbent government three days after an Islamic terrorist strike kills 191 on commuter trains. In response to the strike, the new government agrees to withdraw Spanish troops from the Iraq War.

2006
Rioting erupts in several Islamic countries after the Danish newspaper *Jyllands-Posten* publishes 12 cartoons depicting the prophet Muhammad.

2007
Benazir Bhutto, a candidate for prime minister of Pakistan, is assassinated by Islamic fundamentalists who oppose her moderate views.

1995   **1998**   **2001**   **2004**   **2007**

2000
Seventeen members of the crew of the USS *Cole* die when a bomb detonated by al Qaeda terrorists blows a hole in the ship as it is anchored off the coast of Yemen.

2002
Evidence surfaces indicating that the fundamentalist Islamic regime in Iran is developing nuclear weapons.

2003
An American-led invasion topples the regime of Iraqi dictator Saddam Hussein.

2008
Islamic fundamentalists attack hotels and a Jewish community center in Mumbai, India, taking more than 200 lives. Hindu fundamentalists vow to retaliate.

2005
Eric Robert Rudolph, who set bombs targeting abortion clinics, a gay nightclub, and a crowded park in Atlanta, Georgia, is sentenced to five consecutive life terms. Rudolph was active in Christian Identity, a fundamentalist movement that has targeted gays, Jews, and abortion rights activists.

Related Organizations

American Civil Liberties Union

125 Broad St., 18th Floor

New York, NY 10004

phone: (888) 567-ACLU [567-2258]

Web site: www.aclu.org

The American Civil Liberties Union defends constitutional rights in courts; it has often argued on behalf of plaintiffs who believe governments and others have violated the separation of church and state doctrine of the U.S. Constitution. By entering "church state" in the Web site's search engine, students can find updates on dozens of cases in which the ACLU has taken a position.

American Islamic Congress

1718 M St. NW, No. 243

Washington, DC 20036

phone: (202) 595-3160

fax: (202) 315-5838

e-mail: info@aicongress.org

Web site: www.aicongress.org

Founded after the September 11, 2001, terrorist attacks, the American Islamic Congress is dedicated to educating Americans about Islam. Among the organization's programs are the public education campaign, titled "50-50," which explains the rights of Islamic women.

Americans United for Separation of Church and State

518 C St. NE

Washington, DC 20002

phone: (202) 466-3234

fax: (202) 466-2587

e-mail: americansunited@au.org

Web site: www.au.org

The organization pursues legal cases against American governments that it believes are promoting religious observances and also lobbies legislators to help ensure religious influences are kept out of local, state, and federal laws. Visitors to the organization's Web site can find updates on the group's cases, press releases about the organization's activities, and several essays questioning the motives of religious fundamentalists.

Center for Jewish Studies at City University of New York

365 Fifth Ave., Room 5301

New York, NY 10016

phone: (212) 817-1950

Web site: http://web.gc.cuny.edu

The center studies issues involving American Jews, including those related to Hasidism and other fundamentalist sects. Among the center's activities for the public is a lecture series on Jewish issues. Visitors to the Web site can find a link under "Resources" to the Jewish Virtual Library, which includes many articles on Hasidism.

Focus on the Family

Colorado Springs, CO 80995

phone: (800) 232-6459

Web site: www.focusonthefamily.com

Focus on the Family is a national organization that promotes many issues embraced by Christian fundamentalists, including opposition to gay rights, abortion, and explicit films and music. Visitors to the group's Web site can read a number of essays on issues raised by Focus on the Family and hear a daily podcast by James Dobson, the organization's founder and chairman.

National Academy of Sciences

500 Fifth St. NW

Washington, DC 20001

phone: (202) 334 2000

e-mail: webmailbox@nas.edu

Web site: www.nasonline.org

The National Academy of Sciences was established by Congress in 1863 to give the president and other national leaders advice on matters relating to science. The academy has campaigned against creationist theories of evolution and maintains many resources on its Web site for students to explore evolution and creationism. By following the link for "Evolution Resources," students can read publications supporting the scientific explanation for evolution.

National Constitution Center

Independence Mall

525 Arch St.

Philadelphia, PA 19106

phone: (215) 409-6600

Web site: www.constitutioncenter.org

The museum dedicated to the history of the U.S. Constitution features many exhibits that help explain the application of the Constitution in American society, including issues involving the separation of church and state. The organization's Web site includes an interactive Constitution, in which students can explore the nation's laws by topic or keyword and find links to important U.S. Supreme Court cases.

Pew Forum on Religion and Public Life

1615 L St. NW, Suite 700

Washington, DC 20036-5610

phone: (202) 419-4550

fax: (202) 419-4559

Web site: www.pewforum.org

The Pew Forum on Religion and Public Life studies many issues involving the influence of religion on politics, the law, social issues, and world affairs. Visitors to the organization's Web site can download the U.S. Religious Landscape Survey, the Pew Forum's 2008 poll on American church membership.

Southern Poverty Law Center

400 Washington Ave.

Montgomery, AL 36104

phone: (334) 956-8200

Web site: www.splcenter.org

The Southern Poverty Law Center provides legal assistance to individuals and groups who have been victimized by Christian fundamentalist hate groups such as the Covenant, the Sword and the Arm of the Lord, the Army of God, and the World Church of the Creator. Visitors to the organization's Web site can download articles from *Intelligence Report,* the law center's publication that chronicles its campaigns.

Supreme Court of the United States

1 First St. NE

Washington, DC 20543

phone: (202) 479-3211

Web site: www.supremecourt.gov

The Supreme Court hears cases that determine whether local, state, and federal laws as well as regulations enacted by private organizations and businesses violate the constitutional rights of Americans. Students and other members of the public may attend arguments before the Court, which are usually heard from 10 A.M. to 11 A.M. Mondays, Tuesdays, and Wednesdays from October through April.

For Further Research

Books

Bruce Bawer, *While Europe Slept: How Radical Islam Is Destroying the West from Within*. New York: Doubleday, 2006.

Jimmy Carter, *Our Endangered Values: America's Moral Crisis*. New York: Simon & Schuster, 2005.

Richard Dawkins, *The God Delusion*. Boston: Houghton Mifflin, 2006.

Donna Gehrke-White, *The Face Behind the Veil: The Extraordinary Lives of Muslim Women in America*. New York: Citadel, 2006.

Al Gore, *The Assault on Reason*. New York: Penguin, 2007.

Jay B. Labov, ed., *Science, Evolution and Creationism*. Washington: National Academies Press, 2008.

Stephen Singular, *When Men Became Gods: Mormon Polygamist Warren Jeffs, His Cult of Fear, and the Women Who Fought Back*. New York: St. Martin's, 2008.

Hella Winston, *Unchosen: The Hidden Lives of Hasidic Rebels*. Boston: Beacon, 2005.

Periodicals

Faith Bremner, "Ballot Losses Stun Abortion Foes," Gannett News Service, *Camden (NJ) Courier Post*, November 7, 2008.

Gregory Couch, "Man on Trial Accepts Blame in Dutch Killing," *New York Times*, July 13, 2005.

Steven Heller, "Dialogue: Kare Bluitgen," *Print*, May/June 2006.

Nat Hentoff, "Stoning Women to Death," *Village Voice*, September 26, 2006.

Elliot Jager, "13 Years After the Assassination, Wounds Still Fester," *Philadelphia Jewish Exponent*, November 20, 2008.

Laura King, "Pro-Taliban Commander Is Blamed for Bhutto's Killing," *Los Angeles Times*, December 29, 2007.

John P. Martin, "Prosecutors: That 'Vacation' Was Jihad Training," *Newark (NJ) Star-Ledger*, December 3, 2008.

Jim Remsen, "Religious Leaders Divided over Ideology, Compassion," *Philadelphia Inquirer,* April 1, 2005.

Nicholas Riccardi, "Mormon Church Feels the Heat over Proposition 8," *Los Angeles Times,* November 17, 2008.

Patrick Rogers and Vickie Bane, "Joel Osteen Counts His Blessings," *People,* December 17, 2007.

Jason Tedjasukmana, "Indonesia Tense After Terror Executions," *Time,* November 9, 2008.

Abdul Waheed Waffa, "Afghan Death Sentence Dropped," New York Times News Service, *Philadelphia Inquirer,* October 22, 2008.

Beth Walton, "Protesters Battle over Mississippi Abortion Clinic; Opponents Plan Week of Rallies in Effort to Shut Down State's Last Facility," *USA Today,* July 17, 2006.

Internet Sources

BBC News, "Timeline: Terri Schiavo Case," March 31, 2005. http://news.bbc.co.uk/2/hi/americas/4358877.stm.

Nation, "Religious Fundamentalism." www.thenation.com/sections/religious_fundamentalism.

National Abortion Federation, "Clinic Violence." www.prochoice.org/about_abortion/violence/index.html.

On Point with Tom Ashbrook, "Religious Fundamentalism," WBUR Boston, National Public Radio, October 10, 2005. www.onpointradio.org/shows/2005/10/religious-fundamentalism.

PBS, "A Life Apart: Hasidism in America." www.pbs.org/alifeapart/intro_91.html.

Source Notes

Overview

1. Al Gore, *The Assault on Reason*. New York: Penguin, 2007, p. 48.
2. Quoted in *Daily Mail* (London), "J.K. Rowling Under Fire from U.S. Bible Belt After Outing Dumbledore as Gay," October 28, 2007. www.daily mail.co.uk.
3. Quoted in Colum Lynch, "Saudi Arabia to Lead U.N. Faith Forum," *Washington Post*, November 12, 2008, p. A-11.
4. Quoted in Abdul Waheed Waffa, "Afghan Death Sentence Dropped," New York Times News Service, *Philadelphia Inquirer*, October 22, 2008, p. A-15.
5. Quoted in Beth Walton, "Protesters Battle over Mississippi Abortion Clinic; Opponents Plan Week of Rallies in Effort to Shut Down State's Last Facility," *USA Today*, July 17, 2006, p. A-8.
6. Quoted in *Haaretz*, "Barak: Kadikma 'A Party of Air,' Netanyahu Like 'Santa Claus,'" June 11, 2008. www.haaretz.com.
7. Quoted in Laura King, "Pro-Taliban Commander Is Blamed for Bhutto's Killing," *Los Angeles Times*, December 29, 2007, p. A-1.
8. Quoted in Alan Cooperman, "Is Terrorism Tied to Christian Sect? Religion May Have Motivated Bombing Suspect," *Washington Post*, June 2, 2003, p. A-3.
9. Elliot Jager, "13 Years After the Assassination, Wounds Still Fester," *Philadelphia Jewish Exponent*, November 20, 2008. www.jewishexponent.com.

How Widespread Is Religious Fundamentalism?

10. Daniel Pipes, "Counting Islamists," *Jerusalem Post*, October 8, 2008. www.danielpipes.org.
11. Quoted in Nat Hentoff, "Stoning Women to Death," *Village Voice*, September 26, 2006, p. 20.
12. Quoted in John Tagliabue, "Pope Bolsters Church's Support for Scientific View of Evolution," *New York Times*, October 25, 1996, p. A-1.
13. Quoted in David Warner, "Pope's Study of Church Fathers Not Just for Catholics," Eternal World Television, March 28, 2007. www.ewtn.com.
14. Quoted in Hari Kumar, "India Police Say They Hold 9 from Hindu Terrorist Cell," *New York Times*, November 12, 2008, p. A-6.
15. Richard Dawkins, *The God Delusion*. Boston: Houghton Mifflin, 2006, p. 284.
16. Dawkins, *The God Delusion*, p. 286.

Does Religious Fundamentalism Threaten Individual Rights?

17. Quoted in Reuters, "Veil No Barrier, Says Al Ghasara," *Gulf News*, December 13, 2006. http://archive.gulfnews.com.
18. Quoted in Jewish Telegraphic Agency, "Group Serves Chasidic Dropouts," December 26, 2005. http://jta.org.
19. Quoted in Gregory Couch, "Man on Trial Accepts Blame in Dutch Killing," *New York Times*, July 13, 2005, p. A-13.
20. Quoted in Faith Bremner, "Ballot Losses Stun Abortion Foes," Gannett News Service, *Camden (NJ) Courier*

Post, November 7, 2008. www.courier-postonline.com.

Does Religious Fundamentalism Fuel Violence and Terrorism?

21. Quoted in Will Durant, *The Age of Faith.* New York: Simon and Schuster, 1950, p. 182.
22. Quoted in Durant, *The Age of Faith,* p. 182.
23. Quoted in Walid Phares, "Bin Laden's 'State of Jihad' Speech," April 24, 2006. http://counterterrorismblog.org.
24. Quoted in John P. Martin, "Prosecutors: That 'Vacation' Was Jihad Training," *Newark (NJ) Star-Ledger,* December 3, 2008. www.nj.com.
25. Quoted in Damian Whitworth and Roland Watson, "Fugitive Anthrax Hoaxer Captured in FBI Chase," *Times of* (London), December 6, 2001, p. 18.

How Should Governments Respond to Religious Fundamentalism?

26. Saad Eddin Ibrahim, "Saving Egypt from Mubarak," *Los Angeles Times,* December 10, 2005, p. B-21.

27. Quoted in Ikhwan Web, "Egypt's Muslim Brotherhood Leader Slams President Mubarak's Son," April 23, 2008. www.ikhwanweb.com.
28. Quoted in Michael Sheridan, "We Killed Too Many, Say Bali Bombers," *Times* (London), March 2, 2008. www.timesonline.co.uk.
29. Quoted in Jurgen Kremb, "Indonesia's Secular State Under Siege," *Der Spiegel,* April 6, 2007. www.spiegel.de.
30. Quoted in CNN, "Ten Commandments Monument Moved," November 14, 2003. www.cnn.com.
31. Quoted in Cristina Corbin, "Republican Senator Proposes Amendment to Overturn Ban on Cash for Schools Housing Faith Forums," Fox News, February 5, 2009. www.foxnews.com.
32. Quoted in Danna Abu-Nasr, "Saudi King Shakes Up Religious Establishment," *Philadelphia Inquirer,* February 15, 2009, p. A-4.

List of Illustrations

How Widespread Is Religious Fundamentalism?
Religions in America   33
Fundamentalists Believe in the Literal Interpretation of Texts   34
The 10 Largest Megachurches   35
Lean Support for Sharia Law in Iran   36

Does Religious Fundamentalism Threaten Individual Rights?
Few in Afghanistan Favor a Return of the Taliban   50
Mixed Results on Social Issues   51
Women Are Not Treated as Equals in the Islamic World   52–53

Does Religious Fundamentalism Fuel Violence and Terrorism?
Many Muslims Oppose Suicide Bombings   68
Muslim Confidence in Osama bin Laden Waning in the
    Islamic World   69
Abortion Clinics Under Attack   70

How Should Governments Respond to Religious Fundamentalism?
Support for Military Action Against Iran Declining   85
Should Churches Attempt to Influence Public Policy?   86
Should Religious Symbols Be Displayed on Public Property?   87

Index

Abdullah (king of Saudi Arabia), 12, 75, 84
Abdullah II (king of Jordan), 45
abortion/abortion rights
    Christian fundamentalist opposition
        to, 12–14
    fundamentalists overreach on, 42–44
    goal of criminalizing, 48
    threats to providers of, 67
abortion clinics, attacks against, 61, 70
    (chart)
Afghanistan
    fundamentalism in, 12
    individual rights in, 38
    opinions on Taliban in, 50 (chart)
    Soviet occupation of, 58
        fundamentalist Muslims' view
            on, 14
    support for women's rights in, 49, 50
        (chart)
    Taliban insurgency in, 79
    Taliban takeover of, 37–38
    terrorist attacks in, 56
al-Ahmed, Ali, 11
Aho, James A., 18
Akif, Mahdi, 72
Ali, Ayaan Hirsi, 45
Almond, Gabriel A., 21
American Civil Liberties Union (ACLU), 18
Amish, 7, 62
Amnesty International, 32
apostasy, 46
Appleby, R. Scott, 21
Arar, Nadwa, 29
assassination, as tool of fundamentalism,
    15–17
atheists/atheism, 27

Bader, Eleanor J., 66
Bakalli, Besnik, 59
Balmer, Randall, 47
Banderage, Asoka, 47
Bangladesh, 81
Bar, Shmuel, 64
Barak, Ehud, 15
Beach, Bert B., 29
Benedict XVI (pope), 24–25
Benham, Flip, 13, 14
Bhutto, Benazir, 16–17
Bible, 28
    belief in literal meaning of, 32
        among Protestants, 21, 23
    terrorism and twisted interpretations
        of, 17
bin Hasyim, Amrozi, 72
bin Hasyim, Mukhlas, 72
bin Laden, Osama, 68
    on jihad, 57
    on killing those who offend Allah, 55
    Muslims' waning confidence in, 69
        (chart)
    radicalization of, 14, 58
Blankley, Tony, 80
Bouyeri, Mohammed, 41
Bray, Michael, 65
Britton, John, 61
Bush, George W., 55, 77

Carter, Jimmy, 8, 65
Catholic fundamentalism, 24

Catholics, U.S., percent believing in literal
    interpretation of the Bible, 32
Chechnya, 56
Christian fundamentalist churches
    membership of, 6
    opposition to same-sex marriage in, 49
    preaching message of peace, 62
Christian fundamentalists
    militancy of, 65
    numbers in U.S., 9
    opposition to abortion among, 12–14,
        42–44
    terrorist acts by, 17–18
    views on creation, 8
Christian Identity movement, 17–18
churches, percent saying public policy
    should be influenced by, by religion,
    86 (chart)
church-state separation
    display of Ten Commandments and,
        73–74
    in First Amendment, 83
conscientious objectors, 61, 62

Darwin, Charles, 8
Dawkins, Richard, 27
Demant, Peter R., 46
DeMint, Jim, 75
Department of State, U.S., 67
Duka, Dritan, 59
Duka, Shain, 59

Earth
    age of, 9
    fundamentalist view on end of, 17
Egypt, 58
    Coptic Christians in, 46
    Muslim Brotherhood in, 71–72, 84
Emerson, Steve, 81
evolution
    Catholic position on, 24
    merger of religious principles with, 27

Falwell, Jerry, 71
First Amendment, 82, 83
    evangelicals have benefited from, 47
Fort Dix Five, 58–59
France, ban on religious attire in, 88
Fundamentalist Church of Jesus Christ of
    Latter Day Saints, 76

Gandhi, Indira, 15
Gerson, Michael, 82
al Ghasara, Ruqaya, 39
Goldberg, Michelle, 48
Gore, Al, 10, 71
Grand Ulama Commission, 84
Guinness, Os, 47

Habeck, Mary, 64, 80
Hafez, Mohammad M., 64
Harry Potter books, as target of
    fundamentalists, 10–11
Hasidic Jewry, 22, 25
    women breaking traditions of, 39–40
Haykin, Michael, 30
Herriot, Peter, 30
Hill, Paul, 61, 62
Hindu fundamentalism/fundamentalists,
    26–27

numbers of, in India, 6
homophobia
    link between fundamentalism and, 48
    See also same-sex marriage

Ibn Taymiyya, 58
Ibrahim, Saad Eddin, 71
Ignatius, David, 79
India
    membership in Hindu fundamentalist
        movement in, 36
    terrorist attacks in, 56, 69, 77
individual rights
    in Afghanistan, 38
    in Saudi Arabia, 11–12, 38
    in societies controlled by fundamentalist
        ideologies, 6
Indonesia, terrorism and government
    response in, 72–73
Investigative Project on Terrorism, 81
Iran
    attitudes on U.S. policy toward, 84,
        85 (chart)
    punishment for violations of sharia
        law in, 32
    support for sharia law in, 36 (chart)
Iranian revolution (1979), 23
Iraq
    terrorist attacks in, 55–56, 69
    U.S. invasion of, 59
Islamic Brigade of Shahids, 56–57
Islamic fundamentalists/fundamentalism,
    29
    numbers of, 6
    as percent of international Muslim
        population, 22
    in Turkey, 33
Israel, Jewish fundamentalism in, 19–20

Jager, Elliot, 19
Jefferson, Thomas, 83
Jehovah's Witness, 7, 62
Jemaah Islamiah (Indonesian terrorist
    cell), 72
Jewish fundamentalism, in Israel, 19–20,
    25–26
jihad
    definition of, 57
    moderate Muslims interpretation of, 64
John Paul II (pope), 24
Jordan, freedom of religion in, 45
Justice Welfare Party (JWP), 73
Jyllands-Posten (Danish newspaper), 41,
    42, 49

Kamakhsh, Sayed Parwiz, 12
Kiani, Jafar, 24
King, Martin Luther, Jr., 46
Koresh, David, 60

Lashkar-e-Tayyiba (Pakistani terrorist
    group), 77
al Lihedan, Saleh, 75
Lior, Dov, 19
Lubavitchers, 39

Madrid bombings (2004), 59–60
Mahsud, Baitullah, 16, 17
Martel, William C., 79
Mazahery, Lily, 24

Index

McCain, John, 81
McGowan, Jo, 31
megachurches
  growth of, 22–23
  membership in, 32
  10 largest, 35 (chart)
Mennonites, 7, 62
Moore, Roy, 74, 75
Mubarak, Gamal, 72
Mubarak, Hosni, 71, 72, 84
Muhammad (the Prophet)
  on jihad, 57
  publication of cartoons lampooning, 41–42
  support among Danes for, 49
Mumbai (India) attacks (2008), 26–27, 69, 77
Musharraf, Pervaiz [ED: s/b Pervez], 20
Muslim Brotherhood, 23, 71, 84
Muslims/Muslim world
  decline in confidence in bin Laden in, 69 (chart)
  limitations on religious freedom in, 46
  opposition to suicide bombings among, 68 (chart)
  surveys of
    on definition of jihad, 68
    on women driving themselves, 53 (chart)
    on women making voting decisions, 52 (chart)

Nasser, Gamal Abdel, 58
National Abortion Federation, 67
National Counterterrorism Center, U.S., 55, 56, 67
9/11 attacks. *See* September 11 terrorist attacks (2001)
North, Gary, 21

Obama, Barack, 77, 88
Omar, Mohammad, 37
opinion polls. *See* surveys

pacifists, fundamentalist, 7, 62
Pakistan
  crackdown on Islamic fundamentalism in, 20
  terrorist attacks in, 56
  terrorist camps in, 67
  threat of Taliban to, 77–78
  troops sent after Taliban by, 84
Patel, Eboo, 46
Pew Forum on Religion and Public Life, 21, 27
Pipes, Daniel, 22
Pius XII (pope), 24
Placher, William C., 30
polls. *See* surveys
Pratt, Douglas, 29, 80
Protestant fundamentalists, prevalence of, 21–22
public policy
  attempts by fundamentalists to shape, 42–44
  percent saying churches should influence, by religion, 86 (chart)

al Qaeda, 14, 38, 55
  in attack on USS *Cole,* 14–15
al Qaeda in Mesopotamia, 69
Qur'an
  fundamentalist interpretation of, 10
  on jihad, 57
  on killing of innocents, 63
  message on pluralism in, 46
Qutb, Sayyid, 58

Rabin, Yitzhak, 15
Ramachandran, Sudha, 81
Rashtriya Swayamse vak Sangh (Hindu fundamentalist movement), 26, 36
Ratzinger, Joseph, 24–25
Reform Judaism, 25
religious freedom, limitations on, in Muslim nations, 46
religious fundamentalism
  assassination as tool of, 15–17
  definition of, 6
  government responses to, 7, 18–20, 72–73
  See also specific types
religious texts
  belief in literal interpretations of, by religion, 34 (chart)
  See also Bible; Qur'an
Ridley, Yvonne, 37
Roe v. Wade (1973), 12–13
Roper, Jack M., 11
Rosen, Christine, 28
Rowling, J.K., 11
Rozell, Mark, 43–44
Rudolph, Eric Robert, 18
Russia, terrorist attacks in, 55–56
Ruthven, Malise, 83

Sadat, Anwar, 15
same-sex marriage
  Christian fundamentalists' campaign against, 43
  support for banning, 49, 54
Santorum, Rick, 46
Saudi Arabia, 11–12
  arrests of gay men in, 54
  punishment of women drivers in, 38
  reforms initiated in, 75–76, 84
Scalia, Antonin, 82
school prayer, 18–19
Schwartz, Malkie, 39–40
September 11 terrorist attacks (2001), 7, 14, 38, 55
Seventh-Day Adventist Church, 7, 62
  membership in, 32
sharia law, 9
  fundamentalist interpretation of, 10
  in Iran, 23–24, 32
    punishment for violations of, 32
  support for
    in Indonesia, 35
    in Iran, 36 (chart)
  women's rights and, 45
Shnewer, Mohamad, 59
Sikand, Yoginder, 65
Sivan, Emmanuel, 21
social issues
  support for state referenda on, 51 (chart)
  See also public policy
Souter, David H., 82
Spain
  arrests of Islamic terrorists in, 67
  2004 bombings in, 59–60
al-Subeeh, Nouriya, 37
Submission (film), 40–41
suicide bombings
  in Iraq, by al Qaeda in Mesopotamia, 69
  Muslim opposition to, 68
Sunday, Billy, 8
Supreme Court, on after-school Bible study, 88
surveys
  on Afghans' opinion on Taliban, 50 (chart)
  of Americans

on policy toward Iran, 84, 85 (chart)
on same-sex marriage, 54
on belief in literal meaning of the Bible, 32
on display of religious symbols on public property, 87 (chart)
of Muslim nations
  on definition of jihad, 68
  on women driving themselves, 53 (chart)
  on women making voting decisions, 52 (chart)
  on removal of Ten Commandments in courthouse, 84
  on support for women's rights among Afghans, 49, 50 (chart)
Susskind, Yifat, 48

Taliban, 37–38, 84
  abuse of women's rights by, 44
  in Afghanistan, 79
  Afghans' opinions on, 50 (chart)
Tatar, Serdar, 59
Ten Commandments
  public displays of, 73–74
  views on removal from courthouse, 84
terrorism/terrorist attacks
  against abortion clinics, 61, 70 (chart)
  annual number of, 55
  in India, 26–27
  in Iraq, by al Qaeda in Mesopotamia, 69
  Islamic, motivation for, 57–59
  in Mumbai, India, 69
  number of organizations identified with, 67
Thackeray, Bal, 26
Turkey, growth of fundamentalist Islam in, 33

United States
  Christian terrorism in, 17–18
  Judaism in, 25
  religions in, 33 (chart)
  troop levels in Afghanistan, 88
U.S. National Counterterrorism Center, 55
USS *Cole,* attack on, 14–15, 55

van Gogh, Theo, 40–41

Waagner, Lee, 60, 61, 62
Wahhabism, 11
Wahid, Yenny Zannuba, 73
war on terrorism, is inherently unwinnable, 80
Warren, Rick, 88
Whitehead, John W., 28
women
  acceptance of hijab by, 38–39
  barred from political process in Saudi Arabia, 49
  breaking away from fundamentalist traditions, 39–40
  under sharia law, 45
women's rights
  support for, in Afghanistan, 49, 50 (chart)
  survey of Muslim nations on, 52 (chart), 53 (chart)
  Taliban's abuse of, 44

Zapatero, José Luis Rodríguez, 60
Zardari, Asif Ali, 17
al-Zawahiri, Ayman, 63